FRACTURED MIRROR

BEAUTIFULLY IMPERFECT

Mark Triboulet

Fractured Mirror: Beautifully Imperfect

An Imprint of Ink & Paint Publishing
PO Box 1916, La Mesa, CA 91944

ISBN: 978-1-7352263-6-1 (Paperback)
ISBN: 978-1-7352263-9-2 (eBook)

Manufactured in the United States of America

Library of Congress Control Number: 2020910877 (Paperback)
Library of Congress Control Number: 2020911695 (eBook)

Cover Design: Sharon Marta
Editor: Tiffany Vakilian

Chapter Header Image: Sharon Marta

"The Bricks in My Wall" Image: Pixabay Free—released under the Creative Commons CCo.

FOLLOW MARK TRIBOULET AT:

www.facebook.com/fractured.mirror.5

www.instagram.com/fractured1397

OTHER BOOKS BY INK & PAINT PUBLISHING

Heavenly Ink
by Rikah Thomas

Be at War: Battle for Love
by Rikah Thomas

Loving & Hating This Thing Called Church
by Rikah Thomas

DEDICATION

Without a doubt, this book is dedicated to my beautiful and amazing wife, Laurie, and our five children, Emma Grace, Zachary Wayne, Michael Wayne, Mathew Wayne, and Aubrey Lynn.

Laurie, you, more than anyone, know my heart. You saw in me what I could not see. You encouraged, waited, prayed, cried, laughed, and cheered me on as I fumbled my way through. You never gave up on me, and always believed in me. Thank you, my love, for allowing me to be authentic, even when it didn't look or sound pretty. I am honored to be your husband.

Your life, the way you have lived it, has inspired me. Your natural ability to choose joy and the loving-kindness of your heart spoke words of love to me. Your willingness to not give up on life, especially when death walked in step with you, brought new life to me and those who followed your story. I am blessed to walk this road with you.

My five little monkeys, you tolerated the countless hours it took me to write this book. Not always knowing what I was doing or why, you let me write. Thank you for being patient with me while I was in my writing bubble. I pray you will see all sides of me, and life through this book. Honestly, the glass is not half empty or half full. It is both. You cannot have one without the other. As you already know, it may seem unfair at times, but there are hills and valleys throughout life. Embrace both the hills and valleys of life and give grace to those around you—and to yourselves.

Table of Contents

Introduction

Written over the course of 35 years, *Fractured Mirror: Beautifully Imperfect* journeys through the dreamy darkness of adolescence, the struggles and progression of early adulthood and marriage, to the shallow breaths of life's end.

It deals with love, pain & sorrow, grief, death & loss, hope, God, & Christ Jesus, music, inspiration, marriage, & cancer, walls, mirrors, dreams, & silence.

The "fractured mirror" is me. It's my darkness, loneliness, self-hatred, depression, and anxiety. It is the brokenness in and of me.

The "beautifully imperfect" is what God has created me to be out of that darkness. It is the representation of my wife and her influences in the man I have become.

Fractured Mirror: Beautifully Imperfect is intended to evoke emotion and thought. It is meant to comfort and enrage. It is the dichotomy and fullness of life and death, good and evil...my life.

INSPIRATION

It comes in a multitude of ways.

Love—with its pursuit of chasing and obtaining, its action of choice and denial, and its ever dreamy feelings and ideas—has been a cornerstone of inspiration for me.

As if to counter-balance; loneliness and darkness – with their anger, anxiety, depression, and thundering silence become a cornerstone of the towering wall that inspires pain to become words.

Flowing around and about these two is music.

Music moves me. Whether strings, keys, percussions, horns, or voices, music has long inspired my soul. The rhythms, tones, and space in-between evoke the deepest emotions within me. It's within this realm inspiration breathes.

Family, friends, and life's situations have brought both wanted and unwanted inspiration. Their influence and the stretching of growth and time have inspired unfathomable thoughts and questioning of life.

My Truest inspiration though, has been God and Christ Jesus. Each has personality, traits, deeds, and love that has inspired my heart, mind, and soul. Their love and sacrifice humble me to the point of inspiration. My faith through their inspiration is my foundation.

FRACTURED MIRROR

BEAUTIFULLY
IMPERFECT

CHAPTER I

DREAMING IN THE MIRROR

Going as far back as preschool, I remember being fascinated and enthralled with love and the idea of love. At the innocent age of five years old, my dream of being "in love" began with my first girlfriend, Beth. A multitude of 'dreams' followed. Some floated in on white clouds, while others shook my foundation.

The dream was real.

The dream was imaginary.

The dream was ALWAYS elusive, until the dream stood before me and said, "I do."

SO I WAIT

I feel I am lost
with no one here to help
I feel the need to be loved
but no one stands before me

It's just a phase
some say

To me
it's a neverending tunnel
Or
an everlasting black hole

In reality
the hole is my escape

I have no ladder to get out
Time is too long
and I am too impatient

I grow weaker
every second
as I lose hope and sight of my need

I have been loved before
but now it's gone

Now as I look into empty space
sadly, I say
So, I wait.

Day Dreaming

When I first looked
you were a friend of a friend
just another girl
I thought

I looked again
and now you're my friend,
though nameless
I still looked on

We talked a little
and laughed a little
yet now
you have changed

I looked too much

You were still a friend,
yet this change has
made you beautiful

My eyes and mind deceive me
I look
My mind paints a new picture

I see us walking together
hand in hand
and in love

Reality strikes
when I open my eyes
to see myself in love,
and wanting to be loved,
by you.

Unseen

I look at you
And you're so beautiful.
I love what I see

But you can't see me.

When I listen to you
You talk as if I was not there

And you cannot see me.

I watch you again and again
And all I see are doves
Flying through the sky

Yet you cannot see me.

I touch your lips
As we kiss.

Still, you cannot see me.

I sit here at night
And dream of you 'til it hurts.
I think of how it could be
And then ask myself

Why, why can you not see me?

WHAT CAN IT BE

I never loved her,
Yet there was something

I don't know what it was
Or where it came from,
But it was there

It is not there anymore

And each of us has someone new,
But I feel so strange

Yes, I'm a bit jealous,
But there's something else

If I'm not in love with her,
What can it be

A Kiss is a Kiss is a Kiss

A kiss is a kiss is a kiss
And it doesn't mean anything.
Or does it?

At one time it did,
But that was yesterdays ago.
And I can't live yesterdays.

If I can't live yesterday,
Can I live tomorrow?

If a kiss is a kiss is a kiss,
Then how can I live tomorrow?

But if a kiss was Love

Then I could never die.

IF YOU WERE HERE

If you were here
You could see me.
See me and see you,
Mirrored
In my eyes.

If you were here
You could see dreams,
Dreams that are reality
And reality, that is love.

If you were here
Could I see me?
Or would I see empty dreams?

Sleeping Dream

When I first saw you
You were a dream
Beautiful
A sight beyond my reach

Awakened by your voice
To see the dream was not sleeping

Mirrored images of two
No longer of one

Stretching out for your hands
To find them with mine

It's all about you,
What do you see

Mirrored images of two
Or of one

Is the dream sleeping

I'm wide awake

COULD HAVE BEEN A DREAM IN THE MIRROR

Love between two who are one.
Young in age as in heart,
Yet still in love.

Broken apart
And reconstructed through the years
Has made us strong.
Our love would outlast any other
And withstand the coldest of hearts.

You are my friend,
For that is the strength of our love,
But are you my love?

Could my eyes be blinded
By my own mirror?

Is the mirror darkened by my dreams
Waiting in empty space?

Dreams in the midst become the fractured mirror.

Please help me,
For I truly love you.

What Once Was

What once was
Is now a dream
To dream is to live
But as I know
Living dreams
Is a dream itself

The past was unknown
As is the present now
So, what once was
Is now my dream
And the nightmare
Of my death

A GOOD FRIEND

What am I supposed to say?
Yah, we're just good friends.

How can I lie and deceive you?
How can I lie and deceive me?

Every day I think of you
And every night I cry myself to sleep.

Yah, we're just good friends,
But my dear friend
I love you.

I can't tell you or even
Let you suspect,
Cause if I did
I would surely lose you.

What once was
Is only a kiss by three,
And broken am I
By the third kiss.

What are you so afraid of?
Tell me the truth...

Yah, we're just good friends.

If Only

Destroyed
stuck in my own little
world

Blinded
narrow minded
fool

Yah, that's me
Why must I be alone

The empty feeling won't go away
It has nowhere to go

A heart lost in nowhere

WILL

I can't help it
I can't get her out of my mind
My imagination runs wild
situations, places, and time

All of which, revolve around her

Oh Lord, how will I know?
Will I hear a soft voice
or perhaps a gentle touch
or will it be in the night air
or the morning breeze?

How will I know
when she is love?

Will the dream finally end
or will I dream as I've never dreamt before?
Will the mirror fall
Shatterd
leaving the fracture in a dust of glass?

Will I realize the dream was of man
leaving all eyes on You
and the sight of Your will?

Your will
is my desire
Be it one, or none
Your will, my desire
will be met
if only
I will know

KNOW WHAT I WANT

You said we needed time apart,
to find out what we really want.
By being together
we hurt each other.

The real pain
is going through the day without you.

Without seeing you
hearing you
talking to you.
With only the thought,
the constant thought
of you
flowing through my mind.

If only
to see you.
To see your face
your eyes
see you smile.

With starry eyes
and a smile that breaks a heart,
How could I not know what I really want?

SOMEDAY

How can I hide my feelings,
My true feelings from the heart

My thoughts
My dreams

Are they all meant to be unseen

It hurts me to say hello
And to say goodbye is not to live

I don't want to let you go
But I have to
I love you

Maybe someday...

The Day I Met My Wife

I just met her.

How could I feel so strongly
About her?

Is it her?

The idea?

The dream?

THE TEAR DROP

Like silent rain
The tear trickles down my face.
Why can't you see me?
I'm here, yes, here beside you.

What do you see?
Look through my mask.
Can you not feel my passion?
Don't you see my love for you?

Can you not see my eyes?
See how I look at you?
What do you see in my eyes?

I watch the dream
Over and over again

All I see is you and me
Together

Can you not see the tear
Cascading down my cheek?
It falls like silent rain

I watch you
Walk away

Why can you not see me?

DIFFERENT EYES

How can I look at you?
How can I see you
When I see through different eyes?

My eyes gaze upon you
On your eyes and sweet smile
How could I look upon anything else?

My vision is tunneled
I only see you

You caught my eye
You captured my heart
I held it out for you to embrace
But your eyes said no

As we see
Through different eyes

ONLY YOU, OH LORD

Only You, oh Lord
Know how I feel
Only You can explain
That feeling, that beautiful feeling
Of love

No words
No song
No poem
Can tell of my love for her

Her radiant smile warms my heart
Her gentle voice soothes my soul
Her tender kiss embraces my breath
And her abundant love binds us together

She is all I need

Only You, oh Lord
Know if
I will win her love,
For me

Mystery

Her beauty is far off
Yet I can see her eyes in mine

So plain
So quiet
So exotic
A mystery to me

A dream
Reality
Or only a fantasy

Would fate be so cruel
As to never...

So plain
So quiet
So exotic
A mystery to me

GIFT FOR LAURIE – MY BRIDE TO BE

A hug for the heart of my love
A penguin for your collection

A guitar for *'Always with You Always with Me'*

A phone for the three hours we spent talking
For the first time

A cat's meow for Benny

A CD for the sheer pleasure of music
A note for joyful praise to God

A star of green for Orion and the greatest color
An apple for my favorite teacher

An eye to see, but also to listen to
A stargazer lily for my love

A king for my future wife

A queen for your future husband

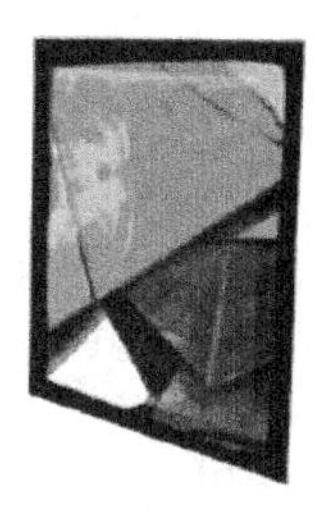

CHAPTER II

CRACKED

The beginning defectiveness of my dream
my life
of me

Loneliness and sadness
medicating into
escapism
anger

A disdain for myself

The first bricks of
my wall

abandonment
anxiety
desperation

So

My name is so
That's all I am, is so
Don't ask me why I'm so
I don't even know the answer to that question

To my friends,
I'm so
weird

To my parents,
I'm so
much like my brother

To my teachers,
I'm so
lazy

To my boss,
I'm so
nice

To God,
I'm so
human

To me,

I am

So

FEELING BLUE

Too much pain
Hurt
Sorrow
Too much time
And not enough joy.

Let Me Be

Sometimes it is better to put on the mask
of a happy face
because when I don't
everyone wants to help

Some may seem nosy and really don't care
those who truly do want to help
seem to be blind or deaf

They say they want to help
but if this is true
why don't they leave me alone?

But no
not them

They have to push
they have to know

Or so they say
it's their right

At these times
I don't care what they say
I want to be left alone

So please
tell them
if they indeed love me
and want to help

Just let me be

19 ON THE 19TH

How depressing,
19 on the 19th
and life goes on

Basically, the dream is dead
Today is tomorrow
as was yesterday

A celebration
or is it just another day
A day filled with basically
and the unknown

Was there ever a dream
or am I the dream itself

Who, what, where, when, and why,
are the greatest of questions
The answers can be found
anywhere but here

How depressing

You ask for a purpose
and you're given a dream
But as I said,
the dream is dead

Does life go on

How depressing

Happy Birthday

It Was Only a Lifetime

The future was ours to hold
while the present is a tassel
now hanging from my mirror

Was it a lifestyle
or perhaps popularity

The people,
clothes, music, cars,
and money

This was four years of
almost totally wasted time

All the rage

All the laughter
All the tears
All the friends

The foes
The memories

All the rage

I must admit, I miss you
I hate you

You are in every part of me
everywhere I go
and in all I write

All the rage

Love and hate

in the same eyes
in the same mind
in the same heart

All the rage

All the rage!

DESTRUCTIVE EXPRESSION

Expressions and actions
are both difficult
and confusing

How does one express
and act
on what he feels
if it is destructive
and wrong?

RUN

You ever just want to run
Run
'til you could run no more?
Run
away from the pain
Fly
Fly away child
high above the pillowed clouds

I live in a world
where I cannot run
'cause there's nowhere to run to

So, tell me

Why the desire to run?

When your friends
don't understand
or don't care
Where do you run?

When you're too old
to run to mommy
Where do you run?

You run in circles
Round and round you go

Where I'll stop

I don't want to know.

Alone

Alone at last
To do whatever I please
Even if it is to cry

Alone I can do
Or
Be anything

Alone I can dream
But
Now I am lonely

No more dreams

Only
Tear
Stained
Eyes

HER

What a fool am I
It's not her.
Only her!

I'll wait forever
and
die a lonely
old fool
for
Her

NO MORE DREAMS

Dreams make the heart
Cold

The mind fills
with apathy
and the soul
slips away

No more dreams

It hurts, Lord

It's too much
Take it away, Lord

End my dream

I plead with you
No more dreams

MISS YOU

Just to talk
To tell you
how I feel
To tell you
how I hurt
How my heart
has been
broken

Just to talk

Will you listen
Listen to me, and listen to you
Can you hear
Hear my cry
for help
The cries
for a friend

For my friend

What happened
Where did our friendship go
And the trust,
Was it all lost behind the tears

I pray God
may heal the pain
And gives us
each other
again

I miss my friend

Isolation

It seems like an old friend of mine now
Heaven and hell
neither stay nor go
just constantly prey and plead
as the heart is destroyed

I look into the eyes of another
and see the love
flow through their heart

My heart skips a beat
and then faster
as I wish it were me

No one feels the crash
when my heart falls and breaks
as the tear hits the wooden floor

Locked away in thought

My heart turns to ice

My world is isolated

Again

Where I'm At

I'm angry
Is it okay to say that
To bring full acknowledgment
of a feeling
that seems to be
socially unacceptable

Without wanting or meaning
to offend
I just want to be human
right now
and express my anger

I don't want to hurt anyone
or anything
I simply want to yell and scream
as I throw my fist
in the air
until I cannot do it anymore

I don't want to tantrum
or overreact
or be told I'm doing so

I just want to express
my anger
And
then
let
it
go

DISTANCE

Your eyes
so enchanting
pierce the stone wall

Your voice
with its soothing sounds
deny the words

Your smile
bright as the day
blackens the eclipse

Your touch
like petals of a rose
tears at the flesh

Your heart
so alive
dies
not for me

From a distance
I am

From a distance
I shall remain
and always be

You
you stand before me

I
at a distance

Wanting Comfortably Numb

I am feeling emotionally overwhelmed
and a bit
defeated too
I don't like admitting that
I'm supposed
to be the strong one
Right

I don't think
either one of us feels
very strong right now
But...okay
I was going to
try and put a positive spin on it
But I won't

This is beyond me
frustration
stress
anger
fear

All the unknown

Not trying to be over-dramatic
But I'm beaten
I long for the medicated sleep that eludes me
I am too tired and drained to write

There are no more words

That Wall

That wall can be used to protect
Keep in
Keep out
Keep locked away

It can be used to say

NO!

You will never pass through

You will never get to me
See me
Hear me
Feel me
Know me

That wall
Built with brick and mortar
Bound together
The razor's edge
That cuts deep

The separation between us

CHAPTER III

BROKEN

The darkness sets in with hopeless silence and suicidal ideation. Death seems to welcome me as a friend as I sink further into loneliness and depression.

I CRIED TONIGHT

I cried tonight
My eyes welled up with tears
of pain
My eyes welled up with tears
of grief
My eyes welled up with tears
of loneliness
They poured out with a sadness
I know all too well

They ran down my face
They covered me.

I cried tonight
In anger
In frustration
In loneliness

I cried tonight
No one heard
No one cried with me
No one cried for me

I cried tonight
The tears have dried
They are gone
But I remember

I cried tonight

STAND OR FALL?

When you feel so low
It's difficult to hold your head up
You look suicide right in the eye

But you must be strong
and say, "No."

Hopeless and helpless,
but you can't seem to do it

You ask for the sight,
another way
Time and patience
as you sit and wait

It's hard not to run away
even though you're doing
what you can

You live your life
day by day
in an attempt
to make your stand

Anxiety

I hate this feeling,
And hate is
a very strong word
The overwhelming sense
of doom
sits slightly above my head

Slams onto my shoulders

It's like the wave
that keeps
pounding you down
and down
And down

Every time I go to stand
it pushes over me
and I fall again

I feel like a baby
or
a little kid
Lost

At times it doesn't seem worth it
to even try to stand

I know I'll only be forced down again

The doom sits
it waits
patiently
for just the right time

When it hits
it hits hard

Fast

out of nowhere
from everywhere

Its power stabs my body
leaving it weak
unusable

It leaves my mind
a pile of mush
unable to sustain
thought

Logic
tossed aside
Amped emotions
run wild
unchecked

A useless pile of mush
is what I've become
I lay there
I waste away

Fear, anger, sadness

frustration

bitterness

regret

all balled together
creating this me
I've become

Overwhelmed with uncontrolled emotions
I shut down
I do nothing
I accomplish nothing
I say nothing
I write nothing
I have become nothing

Nothing

But who
I am

MY HELL

Hopelessness and helplessness
the power of dread and defeat

Hopelessness and helplessness
apathy and agonizing pain
shards of glass
razor's edge
numbed indifference

Hopelessness and helplessness
the place where darkness and death
live and breed

Hopelessness and helplessness
empty, worn out souls
drift away
life slowly slips
shrinking
into the abyss

Hopelessness and helplessness
the absence of breath
the absence of life
the absence of all

The absence of God

Depression

It's that inconsistent rhythmic breath
the sudden start
the sudden stop
the long...
long pause
no air to breathe
no air to escape

that stretched out moment
extending beyond discomfort
drifting
into an unsustainable
unending
unmoving
moment of time

that moment,
that unforgiving moment
of breathlessness
all joy
all peace
all happiness
is
gone

A wave of sadness towers
above
out of nowhere it comes
as it washes over me

The long...
long pause
builds
as my eyes well up

like a vacuum
sucking life and

struggling for breath
I swirl
through swells
and waves
sadness

Tumbling and tossed
in gripping current
knowing not what is up
or what is down

in that moment
drowning

Overcome by its strength
its power
and my weakness
I give in to that
long...
long pause

I embrace the
unexplainable darkness
and lifelessness
of the unsustainable
unending, unmoving
moment of time

I embrace the wave
its swells

and the drowning

I embrace my tears
and breathless soul
in that moment

that unforgiving moment

OH FATHER

All
the anger
the frustration
the feelings and emotions
the confusion between
what is
and what could be

the destructive behavior

and all the sorrow in a
so called normal
depressed
state of mind.

Apathy mixes with anger
and we, that is I,
become lost
stuck in a mind of tunnel vision
surrounded by darkness

Praying for the light of day
praying the tears
will dry
and the test will end

Oh Father, give me strength
to seek Your face and Your perfect will

Tell Me

I'm tired of the silence
Say yes. Say no. Say something. Say anything.
Just speak

Come out of your shell, pull your head out of the sand
open your eyes

Stop pretending you can't hear or see me
I'm not the blank wall
the black demon you portray me to be
I'm not this evil, vile monster preying over you
waiting to devour you and then spit you out
I'm not this mindless, numb, vacant, abyss floating around,
that cannot be

Speak.

Stop pretending I'm not here
Stop pretending
Come out of your fantastical, miserable fantasy
to see me
hear me
Open your ears. Stop plugging them.
Find the breath to form words that communicate

Anything

Tell me to shut up. Tell me to go to hell.
tell me to leave or stay
tell me anything

Just tell me

Bring back the one I once knew
I can't handle this foreign body before me

I don't know her
I don't know you
I don't want to know her
or you

Cold, vacant, dismal, blah

No

I don't want to know you
see you
hear your lies

no more

No More!

AS SILENCE DISTURBS THE NIGHT

lonely is the bed I sleep
lonely is the heart I share
no tears to weep
no hope to bear

like an empty hall
like a barricaded wall
my old friend darkens the light
as silence disturbs the night

shadows of what once was drift
peer through the fractured mirror
broken bloody hands sift
glimmer and bitter

lonely silence of death
disturb and rob each breath
screaming hollow
into tomorrow

Push Me Away

Once, a long, long time ago
I let you go.
No anger, no resentment, no haste.
It was a thought-out decision with no risk
because I was willing
to walk away.

So, I reached out once.
You moved in silent avoidance.
So, I reached out twice.
You moved in uncertainty.
So, I reached out thrice.
You moved in fear. Or so you said.
So, I walked away.

You, sought me out
You, pursued me
You,
You would not let me go.

Now you sit in silent indifference
cold and callous.

I try to hold you tight
but you slip through like sand.
I try to hold you gentle and soft
but you lie limp and lifeless.
I try to hold you without holding
but sleep takes you.

Don't get close.
Push me away.

Close yourself up.
Put up that wall.

Shut down.

Disconnect.

I yell.
I cry.
I beg.
I plead.
I go quiet.
I quit.

Silent is the Night

Silent are her lips
Silent is her tongue
Silent are her ways
Silent is her love

Lonely am I
Lonely are we

Hardened is the heart
Hardened are our thoughts
Hardened are our words
Hardened are our ways

Lonely am I
Lonely are we

The night is quiet
The dawn is haunting still
The day is hollow chatter
The evening is foreshadowing
Silent is the night

Lonely am I
Lonely are we

LONELY IS THE NIGHT

No more tears
No more sorrows
Just a wall of resentment

No more hugs
No more goodnights
Just a valley of indifference

No more I love yous
Just an empty shell

No more words
Just a cold chill of silence

No more hope
Just an empty void

Nonetheless

How sad to look
back through the years
to see such deep sadness
Redundant, yes
but true nonetheless

The silent darkness
seems to have been there from
the beginning
the start
Redundant, yes
but true nonetheless

Glimpses of hope hint
as pierced light
Darkness hides
in the foreshadow
Ironic oxymoron
contradicting the deniability
Of what was...

Or is?

Silent sadness begins
and ends
and begins
Redundant, yes
but true nonetheless

GUARDED HEART

How do I hear when she won't speak?
Listen to her eyes?
But they are closed.

How do I hope?

I can't force change
I can't touch her heart
I can't open her heart

I thought I could. I thought I did.
I was wrong.

It is hers to give
It is hers to hold
It is hers to hide

I was wrong

Forever Foreshadowing

Sitting in secluded sadness

Longing to leave loneliness
watching
waiting
willingly wanting

Tears and fears
full of
leers and jeers

Gloom and doom

All the sorrow for tomorrow

79627

When did I lose you
When did you decide to leave
to disappear

Like the setting of the sun
fading dim light
giving into the night
like the last drop of water
in an ocean that will never quench

Gone

Yesterday seems so long ago
Today just as lonely
Tomorrow?

Does it even exist

Where did you go
Did you drift away with the clouds above
Did you fly away on the wings of a dove or eagle

Perhaps a vulture

Did you sprint away
in a race I did not belong in
Did you become invisible
just as your voice

I miss you

I long to hear your voice again
Wounded with intolerable emptiness
my tears flow nightly into my pillow
They carry the ruin
that is me

What can I say
What can I do
Nothing
The choice is yours

CHAPTER IV

SHATTERED

I feel an evil presence around and about me. It's ominous and menacing. It preys on me and lashes out at me with venomous silence and emptiness. There is no escape. Now engulfed in miserable darkness, I welcome death.

I long for it.

DARK THOUGHTS

do you hear them
what are they saying
do you fear
or are you curious

evil lurks in the halls of our mind
sneering and leering in the corners
shrouded in the shadows
creeping, crawling, clinging to the floorboards
salivating and seeking
to control
to devour

living and breathing
on our
fallen weakness

Anger

I HATE YOUR FOUL WORDS
YOUR VENOM
MALICE
POISON
BITTERNESS

I HATE YOU!

I HATE YOUR THUNDEROUS VOICE
YOUR SUDDEN CRASH
DEAFENING ROAR

I HATE YOU!

I HATE THE STENCH OF YOUR MESSAGE
YOUR SULFUR
PUTRID
CRUEL
EVIL

I HATE YOU!

I HATE THE FEAR YOU INSTILL
YOUR CONTROLLING
MANIPULATING
HEARTLESS
INTIMIDATION

I HATE YOU!

I HATE THAT YOU ARE OF ME.
MY
WORDS
VOICE
MESSAGE
FEAR

I. Hate. You.

WAY OF THE WORLD

trapped in someone else's world
unable to escape
a world that is not of me
but of them
a place that has no place
for me

for I am not of them
I am of God
they are of
the world
their world
not mine

superficial in their ways
trust is scarce
love is unseen
by the naked eye
hate is a door
open to everyone

out of focus
I can't find
my world
or
myself

Death is near

I HURT, SO I HURT

How do I get past this
I don't want to hurt anymore

I hate the empty feeling
inside me
I hate the rejection
the loneliness
I lay awake seething
with anger and bitterness

I want to cry
I want to scream
I want to curl into a ball
and weep
until there is nothing left

Yet, there is
nothing left

No tears come
and the pain just sits there
empty misery

I hurt, so I hurt

I've never done that before
not quite like that

It felt good
It scared me
I wanted to go deeper
and feel more pain

How ironic
using pain
to take away pain

It did not work

I had just as much anger
and bitterness
in my heart
And now
the weight of shame

Awakened by the warmth
hope of a new day
and yet, it remains

Nothing has changed
I've been here before
I should know what to expect
I know how the pattern goes

It's been going for years upon years now
Why would I think it's going to change now
I fight and fight
and then give up
this will never change

Why would it
Nothing is different
same people
same issue

Talk about it
Really
Why
Talk does no good

Temporary band-aide
comes off in a couple of days
Over dramatic
Admittedly yes

But what else do I have
no words seem to sink in
no actions seem to pervade

Stagnant or slowing drifting
I'd say drifting
in the dark
in the light
here, there
nowhere

Does it matter

In a couple of days
it'll be over

The cycle will end
and then begin once again
rejuvenation
followed by a slow descent
into
misery

Drifting...
drifting...
drifting...
lost.

SILENT PRAYER

Sometimes Lord, I pray for death
but I would not have life
if I had death

Only in You, is life
all else is death

I am death

I had life
but then traded my life
for the strong hold
of death

I am death

I want to live
but it's so dark out

Where is the light

hello...

Goodbye

MY DEATH

If someone asks why
I took my own life

Don't tell them because I felt sorrow for myself

Tell them the truth

I hated life

That is
I hated my life

I hated me

I hated
I

Cold and Calloused

Covered with painful needles like that of a dried cactus starved of water
like wood turned to stone over years of hardened anger and bitterness

Don't touch me
Don't talk to me

don't fill me up with your promises of false hope, yet again
let me be
turn from me
walk away

You already have

leave me broken, tired, burdened
empty

You already did

Reaching

The fear of the hurt hovers above
I can see its talons reaching for me
extended just above
reaching ever so closely
Reaching

I can hear its horrifying whisper
scream through my ears
it calls to me
for me
it knows my name
it longs for me

I can taste its bitterness upon my tongue
it swirls through my mouth
it gags and chokes life from me

I can smell its putrid scent
it comes first as a rose to mask what is
but quickly becomes the foulest of foul
I cringe as I gasp for True air

I can feel it shredding me
it pretends to hold me close and securely
but it rips, tears, and lacerates my skin

The hurt is seeping in
whatever cracks may be
It seeps
It envelops
It covers me whole
It takes me within
It has become
me

SILENCE

I heard the echo of silence
I heard its resounding and eerie voice
as it screamed through my bones

It banged its drum through my head
as it trumpeted through my heart
a clashing symbol
a noisy gong
beckoning for a beat

The constant echo
that echoes
more of the sound
of silence
that will not be silenced

the booming volume
that can be heard
By no one

Its vibration shakes the foundation
of my soul
I wail
in its thundering

Silence

engulfing, entrapping, snaring
with the grip of death
Swallowed
by yet even more silence

I long
for a whisper
for even a sound

that could cover
the muffled
sound

of silence

Cover my ears
Close my eyes
Bury my head
No
No

Shhh

don't speak
just hide

Die in the silence
of death

Shhh

Die

SILENT 'TIL SILENT

And you said goodbye to tomorrow for today
as you ignored today for tomorrow
you walk in silence
you live isolated in the imagined tears
tears no one is allowed to see
Where is your rage? Where is your fight?

While death has no sting for you
apathy and complacency have you at six feet
hope has faded into
the fleeting and fluttering
of the very breath daring to escape your lips
Where is your rage? Where is your fight?

Darkness, pain, grief, sadness
Distance, disconnection, disillusion
Solitude, silence, abandonment
Where is your rage? Where is your fight?

Counting the days until the dying of the light
though death has quenched the light dim
dreading the beginning of the end
only to hasten it with indecisiveness and procrastination
Where is your rage? Where is your fight?

Buried deep in thought and sand
Disbelief and Denial
eyes and ears closed off from knowledge and insight
asleep is action
Where is your rage? Where is your fight?

silent 'til Silent

DRIPPING

My skin twitches at the unfeeling, emotionless blade

A moment passes

The blade
sharp and shrill from the somber stone
warmth fills the blade with indifference
as it rests against my skin
comfort and ease beckon the blade in closer

A moment passes

The handle
wrapped leather, frayed, hardened
worn by time
vised with a death grip
or is that a gripping death
Ha, death
calmness settles in as the handle obeys
the idiosyncrasy of its
master
slave

A moment passes

The tip
not pointed and piercing like a skewer
but curved to the left and broken off
fueled by pain and anger
it pounded the floorboards of adolescence
now it's a reminder
of the rage of life, and death

Ha, death again

A moment passes

the fluttering of darkness
the fluttering of light
dripping with penetrating sadness
Dripping

Twenty Plus

I'm tired of feeling lonely
I'm tired of feeling angry
I'm tired of feeling

I want to be numb, cold, and callous
But I can't

It hurts too damn much

What am I supposed to do, Lord

I can't change her
I can't make her love me enough to change
I can't make her show what love she says she has
I can't make her talk or share
anything
I can't make her heart suddenly open
I can't

So why do I try

I play the fool
The jester clown on strings at the tip of her fingers
I dance the same dance for twenty plus
I know each step, each tune, each note

They each end the same
With fingers of silent indifference
Pulling the strings of the bleeding-heart fool

When will I learn
When will I stop dancing, begging, pleading, rationalizing
When will I stop
Lord, make this end

Let these words be the last written

Where is the hope
I wait, not so patiently, but I do wait

How much longer
How long is enough
How long is too long
Twenty plus

Faith
Fleeting

Pain
Penetrating

Sorrow
Surrendered to

Broken
Beaten
Bewildered

Let these words be the last written

It's Cold In Here

It's cold in here
Not like sip on hot cocoa and
sit by the fire cold

No

More like stinging rain
whipping at my teeth-chattering face

It's cold in here
Not like cozy up with
your favorite blanket and book

No

More like bone chilling fingers that just won't thaw

It's cold in here
Not like watching
ever so slightly
falling flakes of snow

No

More like the wind chill that says death is near

It's cold in here
Not like put your hand in mine
and feel the warmth of my love

No

More like dry ice that burns at touch

It's cold in here
Like solid, impenetrable ice
Like thick, frozen steel
Like apathetic indifference
Like hopelessness
Like helplessness

Like
Death

DARKNESS

I laid there staring into the empty blackness. It was strangely cool, like it should be scorching hot or deathly frozen. But it wasn't. So, I laid there.

I felt my eyes lazily sway through the bleak, black, bottomless darkness. It was then that I felt my body sinking. Deeper. Yes, sinking deeper still. The lull of nothingness whispered words ever so slightly in the silence. *Shhhh*

WAIT! NO!

Let me out. Let me out of this darkness. I cannot stay here. I have to get out!

My eyes suddenly and franticly dart from corner to coroner as I feel the searing cold flashes of darkness strike; clawing at me. Shallow is the grave and piercing are the screams of horrifying terror.

Panic. Fear. Dread. RUN!

Running, but getting nowhere. Legs strained. Breath racing. Breath escaping. Weighted down by forces unknown.

Running becomes walking, becomes crawling, becomes trapped. The black sludge about me clings to my feet, refusing to let go. All my strength, all my will, no good. Leaning forward to gain any leverage or ground. Outstretched are the twenty-some arms grasping me, pulling me back.

I feel the presence of evil.

He's there with me. He's clear as day, but I cannot see him.

He's here. With me. Darkened fear, full of malicious evil. I can feel the distain, hatred and the desire to kill. Death and destruction, but that's not all. Torturous devastation. Annihilation. Wretched eradication.

He's moving closer...

Standing before me, beside me, behind me. Enveloping me.

With mouth extended full wide, the silent blood curdling scream is heard

By no one.

Expanded lungs burst into tearful shrieks heard...

Only by silence.

Throat torn. Lungs thin.

YELL!

The moaning gasp of horror resounds and is heard...

As the dreamer wakes with the echoes of
his own terrorized whimper.

My Wall

my wall is cold
blackened and bloodied by silent indifference
layer upon layer
stack the pain, sorrow, and abandonment
sealed and bound together
by years of robotic, emotionless
silence
look closely and you can see the cracks
every crevasse, every fracture
every sign of hope
filled with tears
expound, expand, and exploit them

No!

YOU WILL NOT TEAR DOWN MY WALL!

cold, calculated, and calloused
is my wall
intentional and indestructible
is my wall

before me it rages
beside me it stands
behind me it towers

it is my life giver

and

my life taker

THE BRICKS IN MY WALL

Abandonment Abuse Addiction
All-or-Nothing Anger Anxiety Apathy
Betrayal Bitterness Broken Bum
Callous Cold Damaged Darkness
Death Desperation Depression Disappointment
Disconnection Disdain Disillusioned
Distance Doom Dread Emptiness
Escape Evil Fear Fractured Frayed
Gloom Grief Harden Hatred
Hell Helplessness Hollow Hopelessness
Hurt Ignored Indifference Injustice
Isolation Lies Loneliness Longing
Mask Medicate Misery Old-Self Pain
Panic Protection PTSD Rage
Rejected Resentment Robbed Seclusion Shame
Silence Sin Sorrow Stuck
Stupid Suicidal-Ideation Tears
Trauma Unaccepted Unfair Unjust Vice
Vindictive Violence Void Weary Worthless
Wounded

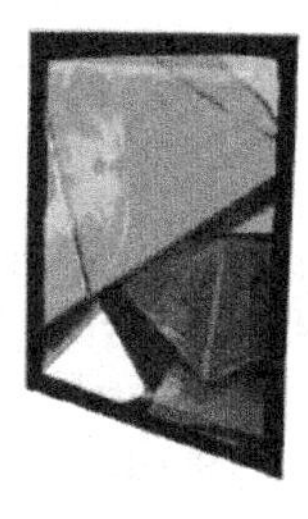

CHAPTER V

IN HIS LIKENESS & IMAGE

From an early age, I accepted Christ Jesus in my heart.
And yet, for many years I did not live for Him. I saw God as the cop waiting for me to mess up, the jury waiting to judge me, and the judge waiting to convict and punish me. It wasn't until later in life that I realized just how loving, merciful, and full of grace He was and is.

I've experienced both hills and valleys in my relationship with Him, but like the prodigal son,

I keep coming home to my Father God.

Like the Good, Good Father He is

He ALWAYS accepts and welcomes me home with open arms.

STATEMENT OF FAITH

One would think that writing a statement of faith would be easy. After all, it is one's faith. Yet I find that this statement of faith is by no means a simple task. It can't just be uttered in a few lines of letters and words to form something so concrete as to say, "This is my all-inclusive belief that has never, nor will ever change."

That being said...

I believe in the Holy Trinity of God the Father, God the Son, and God the Holy Spirit. I believe Christ Jesus was, is, and will always be the Son of God.

I believe God sent His Son, Christ Jesus to live amongst His people to teach them and point the way to His Heavenly Father.

I believe Christ Jesus died as the sacrificial lamb that serves as the one and only acceptable sacrifice for all mankind. It was/is through the sacrificial blood of Christ Jesus that man's sin was/is paid for, allowing man to come before God the Father holy and righteous.

I believe that only through the acceptance of Christ Jesus as one's Savior and God, man's sin is forgiven (past, present, and future). Only then can he enter heaven and live eternally with God, praising Christ Jesus through all eternity.

I believe it is by God's grace man is saved through faith in Christ Jesus.

I believe it is the Holy Spirit that draws man to God.

I believe that, although man is born in the image and likeness of God, man has become depraved due to the Fall through Adam's sin. Because of man's depraved heart, he will not, nor cannot truly seek God without the leading and drawing of the Holy Spirit.

I believe God is the Creator of all this was/is/and will be, and everything is created to bring glory and honor to Him.

I believe God is eternal. He was! He is! He always will be! He has no beginning! He has no end! He is the Great I Am!

The above has not, nor ever will change as God is immutable. But, over the last few years, I have learned so much about my God and Savior. I've learned He is not the abusive or absentee father. I've learned He is not punitive or out to get me. I've learned He is full of grace and not vengeance. I have learned so much about my God and Savior that I cannot write an all-inclusive statement of my belief. I pray I will continue to learn more about Him until He calls me home.

And on that day, I will weep tears of joy as I cry,
"Abba Father!"

Holy as He

My thoughts are dead
My mind is cold
My dreams are shot

Disillusioned am I
In my own head
Heart
Dream

Deep in the memories
Once thought lost
Come the prophetic
Comforting words

"Seek ye first the Kingdom of God"

My life:
It is Yours, Lord
Do what You will
And I pray I may
Become holy as He
For Thou art holy

Anew

Why can't I let go, Lord
Why won't I give it to you
I miss the peace
I miss the comfort
I miss the love

There was once happiness
but now my empty soul aches

A broken heart gathers in desolate misery
and wastes away

My Lord, my God
I need You

Forgive me

My eyes lost focus of You

Cleanse me and make me anew

Love me, Lord
and let me love You

Make me a servant
and I will follow You

SOMETIMES

Sometimes Lord
I just want to be
alone

Alone to dwell in my thoughts
which carry me away
to valleys and lands
where I've never been

Sometimes Lord
I just want to be
alone

Alone I can dream
of what could be
of who I am
and who I want to be

Sometimes Lord,
I just want to be
alone

Alone with you

CHURCH

So after all these years
Was my church wrong
One of my most cherished
possessions or foundations
was wrong

Feelings of
frustration, confusion
denial, anger

Mixed with a desire
to know the Truth
accept the Truth
understand the Truth
as it was written by God

I feel hurt

The church let me down

Therefore...

Let me seek the face of God
The saving grace of Christ Jesus
The heart and soul of the Holy Spirit

DAY OF RECKONING

The day has come
And in my nervousness and fear
I want to say,
"Oh no!"

However, I know my Father in heaven has
already laid this out
and knows the outcome

I know the Holy Spirit comforts and counsels me
with peace
passing all understanding

Christ Jesus is my Savior
regardless of what happens in this world
I will spend eternity with Him

When I look at that last statement
How can I truly be sad

The things of this world will fade away
but my Abba Father is eternal

He was, is and always will be

He is the great I AM

In Him will I trust

Prodigal Coming Home

Even as a believer we can refuse Him
We turn our backs in rebellion
Pretend we can walk away from Him
It's humbling when suddenly
You see how you've been doing this
Over days, weeks, months...
Falling to your knees
You pray for forgiveness
Thanking your God and Savior
Christ Jesus
For never leaving you

I fall
I apologize
I pray
For forgiveness
For my rebellious heart and mind
For the anger and bitterness
I've harbored for far too long
I humble myself before You
My God and Maker
Have mercy and grace on me
Bring me back to a right relationship with You

You are my God

Maker
Savior
Abba Father

You are the great I AM

And
I miss You

Practical Philippians 4:8-9

Let me wake each morning filled with Your Truth
Give me the courage and strength to live
in a noble manner
Direct my thoughts to what is right, pure, and lovely
Focus my eyes to see what is admirable
Let my words be of excellence and praiseworthy to all
Through You
As my day progresses and the night falls
May I walk in Your Truth, putting into practice
Your Word, Your deeds, Your LOVE
The anger, anxiety, and depression
Has plagued my heart for too many years
Let them fall like
Autumn leaves
Winter snow
Spring showers
Summer's radiant sunshine
Let the abundance of joy, contentment, and Your peace
Reign over my mind and heart

****

Philippians 4:8-9 New International Version (NIV)

Finally, brothers whatever is true, whatever is noble, whatever is right, whatever is pure, whatever is lovely, whatever is admirable—if anything is excellent or praiseworthy—think about such things. Whatever you have learned or received or heard from me, or seen in me—put it into practice. And the God of peace will be with you.

PRAYER

Abba Father,
Please bring peace and strength to my family today
as our lives are about to change once again

We ask for comfort and even joy throughout this process

I thank you for the time
Laurie and I had together yesterday

It was good to laugh and cry together

Thank you for my beautiful wife

May all the honor and glory be Yours

In the Name above all names,
Christ Jesus

Amen

BORN

In sweet, subtle, silence
Our Savior was born

With resounding trumpets of victory
Our Savior will return

With all my heart
I believe in Him

With all my heart
I have faith in Him

Do you
Can you
WILL YOU

MY CHRISTMAS...YOUR CHRISTMAS

From yesterday to today
From one extreme to the other
From sinner to saved
Is this not the message of Christmas
Is this not the message of Christ Jesus
From birth to death to resurrection

This is the baby Jesus
Born in a manger
Yet worshiped as the One True King

He stands at the door and knocks

Waiting
Waiting for you
Waiting for me
Waiting for anyone
For everyone
To open the door and invite Him in

My God, my dear sweet Jesus
Please come in

Please live within me
Please rule my heart and my life
I believe in You
You are now my Hope

My Savior

My God

You bring eternal life through
This little baby boy
Born in the manger

Thank You
I love You

My baby Jesus

My Abba Father

WORDS OF LOVE

Words of love are crucial
They often carry us
through the tough times
They lift us and sustain us
in our broken worlds
They wrap around us
and envelop our hearts
Filling us
as we share our love
The greatest Words of Love
I have ever known
And will ever know
Was, is, and will be,
"It is finished."

CHAPTER VI

MY MIRRORED EYES

Standing before me, she my love, my dream –
My Laurel (Laurie) Lynn said, “I do.”

Years of love compounded upon each other from then on with my eyes, heart, and breath mirroring the words, “I love you. AHAW.”

FOR MY WIFE

I love you!
AHAW!

You are my beautiful and amazing Laurel Lynn
NOTHING will ever change that
From the moment I saw you, I knew
I knew I wanted to marry you!

Yes
When I first saw your stunning face
my jaw dropped
But it was your heart I fell in love with
It was
the loving kindness
and sweetness
that is you

I fell in love with
and
wanted to be with
you
For the rest of my life

You are my love
You have True Love Ways

I Love You!
AHAW!

YOU

I woke this morning to hear the sounds of you

The drawers opening and closing
The water running
Hillsong playing

The medicine cabinet
The cough, the sniffle
Even the sound of the tissue

I heard

The footsteps
The stumble of your footsteps

Then
The sweet, soothing sound of your voice

I heard

Whether a word, sigh, a laugh, or a cry
I don't know
I just know it was you

I heard

Did I wake from a dream

Did I wake from a nightmare

Or perhaps I woke from silence

I don't know
I just know it was you

I heard

In one singular, solitary moment

I heard you

Beautiful, wonderful, and amazing

You

LOVE FAITH & TEARS

Ivory keys accompany the fallen drops of tears
tears of joy and comfort
tears of peace and contentment
tears of laughter

Thank you for all the years
all the tears
all the love
all the faith

I love you!
A.H.A.W.

For the Sentimental

For Laurel Lynn Triboulet
For us
For our marriage
For our love
For our children
For the love God gave us
For our future
For death do us part
For the tear running down your cheek
For the glint in your eye
For you
It's always been you
For my wife of 13 years
For my wife forever
For I love you
For AHAW!

POST-OP

Thank you God
for allowing me
more days with my wife

I know she is Your daughter
I know she is Yours

But I count it a blessing
each and every day
I am with her

Thank you for her hand
Thank you for her life

My dear sweet Laurie
Thank you
for coming back to me

Seeing your eyes open
for that split second
filled me up
for too many years to count

I love you

AHAW!

Date Night

I'm going on a date with my beautiful wife tonight.
It still all seems unbelievable, unreal
There are so many things I want to say to her
So much I want her to know
She's still beautiful
She's still amazing
I cannot tell her I love her enough
I want her to see what I see
For me, nothing has changed
I still see my beautiful wife, and always will
For me, what made me weak in the knees
Is still the same
Her beauty runs deeper than just her skin
Deeper than she'll ever know
It's that beauty that drew me in
It's that beauty I fell in love with
It's that beauty I see day in and day out
It's that beauty I long to see
It's that beauty that will always be
That beauty within her...is
It just is
It cannot be changed
It cannot be improved on
It cannot be lost
She will be forever with it
It is within her
It is her
So,
I'm going on a date with my beautiful wife tonight.

FOR YOU

I was sitting here thinking about the last six months
and how life has changed
I never imagined my life would be the way it is
right now
There is still much change to come

Throughout it all I've seen my wife stand strong

She has been a pillar of strength
for me
for our children
Even in her weakness she is strong
much stronger than she realizes

Her strength has been an inspiration
to me
our children
our family
our friends

And to many others that we've never met

I know her strength comes from God
and truly is His strength

And yet

It is her humility that allows
God's strength
to lift her up
and be
a beacon of light

His mercy and grace shines
through my beautiful wife

With each tear shed
He lifts her up all the more
My heart aches for my wife

And yet, I see
how her story
her faith
has touched so many

My Love

A tear trickles down the face of one truly in love
It's the breeze that gently embraces you on a warm day
It's the warmest of warm and the deepest of deep
It's the neverending smile of love
Shining upon the one who is loved

What started as only a trickle
now overflows
With emotion and love for the one

It's that embrace as the sun sets
It's the kiss as the sun rises
It's the peace and security that comforts in the darkness
It's the silent laugh that turns to tears
It's the birth of what will be years before the end
It's the love I still cannot find expression for
It's the beating of my heart when I see you
And I love you, I love you, I love you, like never before!

Thank You Laurie

I am honored to be your husband
I would be lost without you
I am in awe of the beauty that God has given you
you radiate His love and His grace

You radiate

Even now with all that has been lost
you are complete
you are whole
your heart is with Him
just as it should be

I can never say I love you enough
I can never show it enough

I will spend the rest of my days
trying to match your love
and likely fail because it is who you are
and I cannot compare

But
I will be here trying each day
to show my love for you.
For you
I love you
I love you
I love you
Like never before
Like never before

AHAW!

15 YEARS AND COUNTING

Fifteen years ago
today
God blessed me
by giving me my best friend for my bride
Little did I know how deep my love for her would grow
She has seen my highest of highs
and my lowest of lows
and still loves me

She has lifted me up and carried me
through more than I ever wanted to go through
She has encouraged me, praised me
been my cheerleader
even when I didn't want one

She is the shining star in my life
She is the brightness of my day
and behind my every smile
Never would I have known, the trials we would go through
From addictions to breast cancer
and yet, here we stand united together

For better or worse
For richer or poorer
Until death do us part

Now, after a mastectomy
losing her hair
giving birth to four children
and now eight months pregnant
with our fifth child
I look at my bride
I have never seen her look so beautiful

She shines
She radiates with beauty

her smile
her eyes
and her beautiful bald head
All resonate the beauty that she is

She is my bride
She is my best friend
She is the mother of my children
She is my life
She is Laurel Lynn Triboulet

Happy 15 Year Anniversary Babe

I love you!

AHAW!

40

It's difficult to know what to write
for a birthday I know you don't want to have

A year ago we celebrated your birthday
without a care in the world
We had life's general concerns
children, finances, and schedules
but nothing we couldn't handle

Our lives seemed so much simpler then
though we had no idea just how simple it was

A year later
Wow
need I say more

It was just four days after your last birthday
your life
our lives
changed in a way that we could not have imagined

We did not know it,
nor want it to,
but it changed us forever more

The pain, grief, sadness, and utter disbelief
have sat upon our shoulders
for what seems like so long now
This new life has brought us to our deepest of depths

It has also given us new blessings
beyond our heart's desires
As we come into this new day
we put an end to yet another chapter
(radiation)
in this new life

I would imagine this day is bitter-sweet for you

You've made the comment a couple times
this past week
that you don't want to be forty
and don't want to be that old
or old at all

When you stand before me
I don't see a forty-year-old woman
I still see the beautiful face that captivated me
twenty-some years ago

I still hear the voice
that sooths the stress and worry of my heart
I still smell the exotic scent that draws me to you

I still taste the sweetness of your kiss
I still touch the beauty and fullness that is you
I still see the woman that I want to grow old with

I still see us forty years from now
with our backs arched and a couple inches shorter
walking hand in hand to get our smoothies

Even then, I will still see the beauty that is you
None of this may make turning forty any easier for you

But know that I am there with you
every step of the way

I love and adore you
AHAW!

LAST

And on that day

The day I breathe my last

I will thank my God and Savior

For the life He gave me in you

When

when does
the intoxication of your smile
fade
when does
the sun cease to shine
in your eyes
when does
your fragrance
allure me not
when does
your reflection
reflect anything but beauty
when does
your voice
not skip a beat of my heart
when does
the kiss of your lips
wane from my memory
when does
the washing over of you
melt into the washing over of me
when does
the love of what is
become the love of what was

IN SILENCE

In silence we said hello
In silence we shared
In silence our bond grew

In silence we stare
In silence our eyes locked, unmoving
In silence I see the beauty of you

In silence we breathe as one
In silence our hearts are held
In silence they beat

In silence fingers entwined
In silence we stood
In silence we are held

In silence we walked
In silence filled with laughter and tears
In silence we are one

In silence we speak
In silence words are heard
In silence we feel

In silence we knew
In silence we loved

In silence

We say goodbye

FOR MY BEAUTIFUL WIFE

I love you dearly
Please rest in His arms today
Take comfort that
our Lord
God
and Savior
Christ Jesus
is walking this road
with you

He knows the bumps
the twist and turns
the hills and valleys
and even the end

He knows

He is here

He is with you

He loves you!

By no other Name

A MOMENT

I was sitting outside today, enjoying the pool
Laying in peace, in the warmth of the sun
There was a calm in the air that swept over me
I felt relaxed

My heart and mind were composed
As they took in the solace of the moment
And then the moment was gone

Tears filled my eyes
Grief set in
Turmoil swam
In me

You flooded my mind
The memories and what was to be, covered me

There, standing before me was you.
All I could see was you
Everywhere I looked
You were there

I heard the softness of your voice
Your laughter surrounded me
Echoes of you resounded through and through

So sweet was your voice
So right and perfect

Overcome by
Emotions I did not want to feel
I closed my eyes

Tears filled my eyes
Grief set in
Turmoil swam
In me

I sat there in silence
Sat, waiting for the moment to pass
Yet, in vain I waited as the unmovable moment refused
It taunted me as my shoulders shook
With pain and more tears flowed
In knots, my stomach ached and begged
For the moment to pass
End

Just end

Tears filled my eyes
Grief set in
Turmoil swam
In me

How do I not see you there
I open my eyes, I close my eyes
My eyes are swollen with pain of burning tears
I open my eyes, I close my eyes

Where are you

You were just here
Where are you
Everywhere I look, you are there
And yet, you're not

I cannot see you
I cannot hear you

Where are you

I want to see you just one more time
No, I want to see you forever and never not see you

Tears filled my eyes
Grief set in
Turmoil swam
In me

27 YEARS AGO

We started a lifetime
Not knowing what we would see
do
experience

We still chose that road
and each other

Today and every day

I would still make that choice

I love you more than ever

My Laurel Lynn!

UNEXPECTED

Unexpected
you walked into my life
dull and non-descript
Until I met you

Unexpected
you joined me in life
meaningful, purposeful, colorful, and full
Step by step, we walked

Unexpected
you gave us life
five beating hearts
Crawling, walking, running, driving, leaving

Unexpected
cancer took hold of life
hills and valleys of unknown
With bowed hearts and bended knees
we lived

Unexpected
you ended life
torn in two
But
Cherished because I met you
I walked with you
I loved you
And
Lived life with you

FOR

for my wife
for my friend
for my love
for my best friend
for the mother of my children
for my beauty
for the one that loves me
like no other
for the one that did
what no one else could do
for my thankful heart
for my wife
Laurel Lynn Triboulet!

Last Night

I held you in your sleep
I stroked your head as you laid there still
In my sleepless night, I held you

Thoughts of you
Thoughts of me
Thoughts of us together
Each frame pictured by overwhelming joy
A tear welled up as I laid there
You and I

I held you as you breathed in
I held you as you breathed out
Overcome with love
I held you

My love
My sweet, sweet love
How long may I hold you

My eyes grow heavy
My breathing slows
My mind drifts through the love of you
As I hold you still

Never to end
Never to sleep
Never to wake
I will hold you
As I held you last night

WASTED LONGING

How many wasted days
How many wasted nights
Weeks
Months
Years

For so long, I longed
too long

Wasted were the words, tears, and torn hearts
the joy and contentment
wasted by the anger

Longing for what was right before me
but too blind to see
but too deaf to hear
but too silent to speak

Wasted by stubborn arrogance
Selfishness
Pride

Wasted time and regret
Missed blessings of peace and harmony

Oh
to take it all back
to start over
to have a redo
to see you as I see you now

Today
On this day
Yes, this very day
I have today

Today is as tomorrow as was yesterday

No
Today
I have today
We have today

Today
I am with you
With you,
By your side
I will be

BEAUTIFULLY IMPERFECT

I see the broken pieces of your heart
once whole, beating steadily
soft, gentle, and sweet
full of life-giving love
full of hopes, dreams, and peace

Smooth and soothing was your heart to touch
enveloping, encouraging, and empowering
were the words of your heart

With intoxicating wonder and love
the eyes of your heart looked out
comfort, calmness, and quietness
breathed life into and from your heart

Now lay fragments of fractured glass
thrown about here and there
Randomly. Haphazardly. Chaotically.
Broken pieces skewed about like shattered glass
Edges sharp and bloodstained by timeless sorrows

Etched deep are the blackened scars
of life's pain, agony, and regret
The heart gasping for air
now grasping for life

Breathe

Hear the heartbeat that still beats

Breathe again

Take a step back
And look
See with new eyes

Your heart
Beautifully cracked
Beautifully chipped
Beautifully cut

Beautifully you

You are the stained-glass window of my soul

We

We said hello never wanting to say goodbye
we whispered I love you because we always had
we walked hand in hand and cried each other's tears
without limits, without boundaries
we breathed deep the life we built
home with you
home with me
home for us

Raining down before us
the hard truths poured over us
drenching, soaking, flooding
about us

We, yet together
we stood

Bound by a covenant we vowed before God
we two flesh, became one
we for His honor
we for His glory
we for His pleasure
we
ordained
by
Him

I DO

One true love
God joined us together
Two flesh became one

Our covenant
No man will asunder
Only death will part us

I will spend the rest of your days
I will spend the rest of my days
Loving you

Marry me

A GIFT FOR LAURIE – MY BEAUTIFUL BRIDE

A bell for our wedding and your resounding joy
A church to plant roots
A Sunday School to do life with
A Hillsong for your heart, soul, and mind
A hail/hell to bring much needed laughter
A vase of picked flowers for May Day
A TV for *Friends* and *Survivor*
A dress made out whatever is lying around
A DVD for *Some Kind of Wonderful*
A Netflix and Amazon for binge watching
A text, emoji, or gif just to say I love you
A deck of cards for Nertz
A crazy cat lady
For Bernie, Buddy, Holly, Socks, Mo, and TJ (or Chloe)
A litter of children
(Emma, Zachary, Michael, Matthew, Aubrey)
To go with the cats
A razor for your head
A laptop for your chemo days
A Kleenex box for your tears, and mine
A pool deck and beach to relax in the sun
A lifetime coupon for Pepsi and pizza
A home where there is peace for our souls
An I love you
An AHAW because I AHAW

CHAPTER VII

HER MIRRORED EYES

Laurie truly captured my heart from the moment I met her. I can't explain it, but it's real. While soft-spoken, she has a depth to her heart that I longed for. The following is a small example of her heart. This chapter is comprised of Laurie's poems while we dated.

This chapter is for my amazing and beautiful wife.

You have True Love Ways.

I love you

AHAW!

Two Hands

Two hands...They touch
Two hands...Pressed together
Two hands...Can't let go of each other
Two hands...Won't let go

It means too much

Laurel LePere Triboulet

TWO LIPS

Two lips meet,
What does it mean?

Two lips join,
What does it stand for?

Two lips come together,
Why does it happen?

Two lips brush against each other;
They are ours.

Why do I like it?

Two lips together,
It is precious;
It is sacred.

Will they meet again?

Laurel LePere Triboulet

IS IT WORTH IT?

Emotions are fighting back and forth inside me,
like a bloody war.
do I like him?

Is this worth it?

Words are tossed back and forth between us,
like the stormy ocean;
should we give up?

Is this worth it?

Love is shared back and forth among us,
like a warming fire,
should we try?

Is this worth it?

Time is passing by
like a distant ship;
should we rush it?

Would it be worth it?

Friendship swells within our hearts
like the golden sunshine;
should it continue?

It is priceless.

It is worth it.

Laurel LePere Triboulet

Lips

...will they meet again?

As the sun meets the horizon,
so will our lips meet again.

Laurel LePere Triboulet

SLIPPING AWAY

Anger
Bitterness
Strife
Why does it have to be like this?

Yelling
Attacking
Accusing
Why does this exist?

Ignoring
Avoidance
Tenacity
When will we mature?

Hurt
Resentment
Pain
Why won't it cease?

Love
Understanding
Trust
Why can't it be like this?

The desire burns inside

What if it's too late?

What if we have slipped away...

Forever?

Laurel LePere Triboulet

SHOWERED WITH PAIN

Showered with pain
the hurt overwhelms me.
My heart cries out
with a silent scream.
I try to continue
but only am hindered.

How can I go on
when while standing, I fall?
To be able to go back
and try to relive it;
To undo the pain
and the hurt that I've caused.

I cry out, "I'm sorry"
these words are not empty

I cry out, "I'm sorry"
cuz that's all I feel

My body is numb
and my heart's being eaten
by the pain which, like acid
burns my sanity away

Showered with pain
the hurt overwhelms me
only to hope
for the pain to subside.

Laurel LePere Triboulet

EYES

There are eyes that watch me
but do they really see?

There are hands that touch me
but do they really feel me?

There are people that know about me
but do they really know me?

There are ears that hear me
but do they actually listen?

There are arms that hold me
but do they actually carry me?

I look for someone who will see
feel
know
listen
carry me

But will I actually find such a person?

Does he exist?

Am I asking too much?

I know he's out here somewhere...

Perhaps
much closer
than I'd like to admit

Laurel LePere Triboulet

TOGETHER

After the discussion comes to a close
we find ourselves lying side by side

You hold me so securely
as your strong arms pull me close to your side

The sound of your breath whispers in my ear
with each sigh of contentment

My head rests gently on your chest
able to hear the rhythmic beating of
your heart

Lying side by side, I think about us

The moments we share

I am lost in these moments

When I awaken
I find
we are still lying

Side by side

We are together
in this solitude

Laurel LePere Triboulet

Rain

Here I am
again

Broken
Shattered
Ripped
Torn

Where should I go
Which way should I turn
Should I go right
left

But then there's up
down

My mind is spinning
in a
nightmare

I can't focus
I can't think straight
I just want him back

He was with me

Why did he have to
leave

If it wasn't meant to be
why are we so confused

I want to try again.
does he

I miss him.

Does he miss me

If you can hear me

Come back

Laurel LePere Triboulet

Nothing Left

My life begins
My heart is weak
With each breath
It is strengthened

As I get older
I sense new emotions
With each day I become stronger

I live my life taking care of myself
Trying not to let anyone take advantage of me

As I try to become stronger

I have failed

With each relationship
My heart is ripped apart
It heals, eventually
But not as strong as it used to be

Each new relationship
Breaks open the old wound

Soon. I will have nothing left to give
My heart has been
Shattered
So many times
The pieces will fit together
No longer.

Laurel LePere Triboulet

FROM A DISTANCE

Each day passes by
it's supposed to get easier
I try to forget you
but my feelings endure

Across the room, I see you there
Eyes watching what goes on around you

From a distance
they meet

And the world stops around us

My heart races
As you sneak a smile
"I can see it in your eyes," you say

But be careful—
I can see your eyes too

Laurel LePere Triboulet

Chapter VIII

Little Shards

Never would I have imagined Laurie and I would have five children. They have been such a blessing and I dearly love them.

Never would I have imagined our five children would have to endure the years upon years of watching their mom go through chemo, surgeries, radiation, hormonal treatments, and still more chemo. They've watched the slow descent of their mother's energy and life and the multitude of hills and valleys that cancer brings.

My dear littles—my little shards—they've ridden a rollercoaster they never wanted or deserved. Their pain cuts me to the core of my essence. Their strength inspires me.

This chapter is for them and by them.

My Little Shards

My Life

My life is a crazy rollercoaster
bringing me ups and downs
but mostly downs

A Mom with cancer
annoying siblings
trust issues with friends
and many more things

But what gets me through it all
Is music

If music wasn't a thing
I really don't know how I would still be alive

Music is the food for my body everyday

Emma Grace Triboulet (15)

GOING NOWHERE FAST

You drove me here alone
Music blaring through the windows
Everything left my mind
All my thoughts were drawn to you
Don't care where we go
Don't care what we leave behind
Going nowhere fast

I don't know how to feel about it now
Just get out of my head
Just leave me alone

We talked all day
And talked all night
Our voices hoarse, going out so fast
Make it go on forever
Make it stop
Going nowhere fast

I don't know how to feel about it now
Just get out of my head
Just leave me alone

We walked all day
Fled the night
I lay in your arms
Your soft words tingling my ears
Don't wanna go
Don't wanna stay
Going nowhere fast

Emma Grace Triboulet (15)

I LOVE MY MUSIC WHEN...

I love my music when it's loud
I love my music when it's intense
I love my music when it's crazy
I love my music when I can feel the beat in my chest
I love my music when it takes over my body
I love my music when it takes over my mind
I love my music when it fills me up
all the way with its sweet goodness

I love my music when nobody's home and I can be me
I love my music when I can act exactly like the singer
I love my music when I can sing just like they sing
I love my music when I can sing out the words
with all my heart and soul

I love my music when I can be me
and act out any words I want

I love my music when I can calm down
from anything I was feeling before

I love my music when it makes me feel alive

I love my music when...

Emma Grace Triboulet (15)

Him

His scratchy blond hair
floating in the wind
His bright green eyes
pierce right through my gray eyes
His big soft hands
tangled in my small pale ones

Emma Grace Triboulet (15)

Chill

How would you define chill?

I think of a person
who is awesome to be with

I am that type of person

Just like the sun
The planets love to hang with the sun
And how the people on Earth cherish the stars
Like the comets embrace the open space

Chill is how I see myself

Clinging to my friends and family
I love so much
as I go through my everyday

I am chill to be with
'Til the very end

Zachary Wayne Triboulet (13)

LIFE

Life is full of ups and downs

But through it all
I am always up
I don't always feel up
I act like I am up
though I am down

Life is full of ups and downs

Cancer is one of those downs

I keep all my feelings inside
but I need to get them out
I keep them inside
at night I think of life
without cancer
Boy, it would be another story

Life is full of ups and downs

Eight years is one of those ups
I am sooo happy for the eight years

I've been blessed to still have my mother
Eight years since her cancer started
Eight years since my mother was
blessed by God in billions of ways

I love her sooo much!
I hope she is okay for another eight billion years

Zachary Wayne Triboulet (13)

Death

Death can mean different things
Like no longer living on Earth

But the way I
See death is
Sadness, funerals,
Crying, gravestones

Death can be sad
And depressing

Death is like a stab
In the heart with a sword

It would be nice to get
An award for death
'Cuz it happens so often
But that's just not the case

I know death hurts
But it's just part of life

Zachary Wayne Triboulet (13)

HELP!

"You need help."
is what many people
say to me

Do I really need help?

We all might need help
if you think of it like that

Sometimes I think I need help
Sometimes I just want to scream
"HELP!"

But no one will hear me
because I am in a room
all alone

There is no one there to help me

I just make myself curl into a ball
and hide in the corner of the room
I wait 'til I can see
the sun shining again

Sometimes I think
What if I do need help?

Do I want help?

I am not comfortable
talking
to someone I don't know too well

But what if it's time
to get out of my comfort zone
and talk to someone

and get help like
those people are telling me

What if they are actually
telling me to get help.

Should I listen to them?

I feel like I should
but I don't want to

I need some time to think

Zachary Wayne Triboulet (13)

SCHOOL

School is so boring

I mean,
all you do is listen to the teacher
and do your work

So boring, right?

The most fun thing is
break and lunch.
On Wednesdays, I usually get pizza
and I enjoy it

On Tuesdays and Thursdays
I sometimes get a snack
from the Snack Shack—
other than that school is boring

I am happy when I get a good score on a test
10/10 is what I always aim for
but I usually get an 8/10 or a 9/10

My friends are awesome
fun to be with

My friends have fun with me
We die in laughter
We mess around in class
We have a good time
but when we take it too far
we get in trouble
But in the end, we don't usually regret it

School is boring, but fun

Zachary Wayne Triboulet (13)

One Thing

There is one thing
I want right now

Can you guess?

Yes,
it's peace

Peace is something
I've NEVER had before

But if I ever have peace
I will use it to my advantage

This one thing
something
I have been wanting
for as long as I can remember
I think for eight years

Eight years
since
there was no peace

No peace means that
wicked things
could and
more than likely
will happen

This one thing

Peace

something I need
something needed

for all of us

Peace
something that
will never come
But something
I want

Zachary Wayne Triboulet (13)

WHAT DO YOU SEE IN ME

What do you see in me?
I hope you see something good

'Cuz if not I don't know what I would do

What I see in me
is a guy who just wants
to make his way in life

I hope that's what you see

What do you see in me?
I hope you don't see my dark side
It's not what you want to see

I hope

If you want to see my dark side
make me FURIOUS
you'll see my dark side

But I want you to see my bright side

What do you see in me?
I hope you see that I am a funny guy

That's what I see most of the time

Other times you might see
I am

the saddest guy alive

Zachary Wayne Triboulet (13)

IS IT JUST A DREAM

What would begin my life of beauty and adventure? Going to Disneyland? Going on vacation every now and then? Living in Hawaii? Going to Disneyland that would bring joy to my heart. A vacation would bring some beauty and adventure, and living in Hawaii would bring the rest.

Then my heart is ready for the party!

I want to go and see the world. I want to see the northern lights flashing like fire. I want to see the beauty of Niagara Falls. I would love to eat the chocolate from Hershey, Pennsylvania and visit the Alamo. When I'm in New York I would see the towering Statue of Liberty and take a tour on Ellis Island. I want to see the ancient buildings of Italy and Rome.

What's in Mexico and Russia? I want to find out.

I would love to explore Australia. And when I try to fall asleep in Africa, I would hear drum beats and howls from African tribes. I want to have fun at Disneyland. I want to freeze my body in Greenland and Iceland after dragging myself out of Death Valley.

I want to live my life!

For my future, I would have two to four kids. I would be rich and live in a big house in Hawaii. I would be famous and change the world. I would change others' lives. I would be joyful and happy. And as the days go by, I would go on vacation now and then.

I would live a good life.

In my future, I would change the world of art. Such things would make my life a dream. My life would be so good and rich, like chocolate. And the nightmares would be impossible to have. Unless, it's all just a good dream.

Michael Wayne Triboulet (12)

SUGAR

Oh, the sugar
the sugar in candy
the candy my kids eat
the candy that makes my kids hyper

Oh, the sugar in cereal
the cereal my kids eat
the cereal that makes my kids wired

Oh, the sugar in food
the food my kids eat
the food that makes my kids full

Oh, the sugar in life
the life I have
the life that makes me laugh and cry

Oh, the sugar in joy
the joy I have in my life

Oh, the bitter sugar in sadness
the sadness I have in my life

Oh, the sugar in life
the life I have

Michael Wayne Triboulet (12)

---

[1] "Sugar" is inspired by a big bag of candy that our generous neighbor traditionally gives to us on Halloween.

THE PETALS OF A FLOWER

The petals of a flower
are like life
When a petal falls or dies
it's someone dying
When one is created
a baby is born

Life is like the petals of a flower

Michael Wayne Triboulet (12)

The Rich Ones

There are a lot of poor people
There are a lot of normal people

And some rich ones

Some people deal with things
Like a sickness and cancer

The rich ones

The rich ones don't help the poor
They don't help the sick

And they don't help the ones who deal with
sad and harsh things
like cancer

It's frustrating

They're rich

Donate money
They can help cure the sick and the ones with cancer
but they don't

They're too caught up in being rich
They can't open up their eyes
and see what people are dealing with

They're so caught up in it
they can't help
They just leave them helpless and sad

If I were a rich one, I would help
I would donate money

I would support others
because I know what it's like

Since 2011 my mom has had cancer
eight years
I have only known my mom without cancer
for four years

The rich ones

Don't help
Don't donate
Don't support others

They keep their eyes closed
They're dreaming of nothing bad

No one sick
No one poor
No one suffering
No one sad
No one depressed

That's what the rich ones do

Nothing

Michael Wayne Triboulet (12)

---

[2] Michael wrote "The Rich Ones" from the frustration and sadness of watching his mom struggle with cancer for the last eight years. He has such a generous heart and believes people should give like he does/would. While still young, he does not understand yet just how blessed we have been by "the rich ones." He just knows his mom still has cancer and is dying.

A Poem About what to Make a Poem About

It's hard to make a poem
First, you have to think
of what the poem
is going to be about

Then you need an inspiration

It's hard to think
of what to make a poem about

There are so many choices!

Hmmm...
What to choose, what to choose

Oh!

I'll make a poem about
what to make a poem about

That wasn't so hard
after all!

Michael Wayne Triboulet (12)

ISN'T

"Isn't" isn't a word we use a lot

Or is it

Let's see
Isn't hot chocolate mix better than hot chocolate
Isn't Elmo and Sesame Street for little kids
Isn't junk food bad for us
even though adults eat a bunch of it

Isn't loud music bad for our eardrums
Isn't the splits easy for girls, but hard for boys
Isn't kissing on T.V. gross and disturbing
Isn't it annoying when your siblings
are loud and obnoxious
for no reason

"Isn't" isn't a word we use a lot
Isn't the answer yes

Told you

We use isn't a lot these days
don't we?

Michael Wayne Triboulet (12)

TJ

TJ, oh the adorable cat
the fluffy little kitten, TJ.
how all of the family loves him
except for my Dad

He loves to purr in
and under
all the beds

He makes the weirdest meow
you will hear in your life
he will snuggle in your bed
stay there and think

"Wow I love my life and I will stay here forever"

Matthew Wayne Triboulet (9)

TRUTH

3. . .2. . .1. . .

Cancer sucks!

Matthew Wayne Triboulet (9)

The Mystery Books and Bad Books They Read

Once upon a time, there was a girl
She lived in a cottage
and her mom was very sick

One day the little girl became sick
and it was very sad

She and her mom did not feel very well

No one felt good
Her dad did not feel well
It was really not good
Her sister did not feel well
Her brothers did not feel well
and it really wasn't good

The End
clap clap clap clap clap clap clap clap!!!!!!!!!!!!

Aubrey Lynn Triboulet (7)

T.J.

I love T.J.
He is funny and cute
He likes to play with strings
He likes to lay in Emma's chair
He LOVES to get flies on windows
And when they are flying around the house
He loves my pillow that has cats on it and it is cute

Aubrey Lynn Triboulet (7)

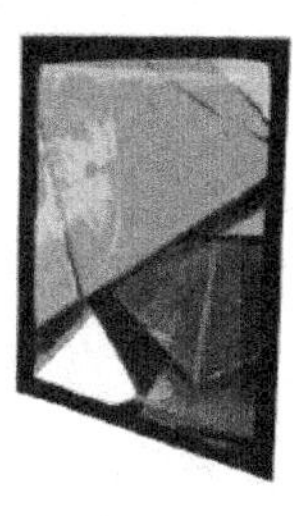

CHAPTER IX

REFLECTIONS

My wife can always tell when I'm deep in thought.

My head tilts slightly to the left and my eyes stare far off, as if searching the stars beyond my view. The left side of my brain philosophically questions life and its wonders.

All the while, the dreamer, full of grandeur, resides outside the box in the right side of my brain. His emotions and passion run deep—a bit deeper than his counterpart.

DREAM OF HOPE

The answer is in a dream
my friend

dream on
let your mind race
wander, and roam
all your
ambitions

Don't give up
my friend

don't lose hope
don't throw it away
before you receive it

let your mind be filled with dreams
and your heart with hope

Hope for today

Hope for tomorrow

Hope for God

Pondering

Pondering how
Lucifer
Adam
Judas
all were in the actual presence of
God the Father
and/or
Christ Jesus

and in their pride
blew it

Yet

how am I any different

WILL I

Can I follow
my own advice

Can I breathe
through the pain

Can I breathe
through the anger

Can I breathe
through the tears

Can I breathe
forgiveness

Can I take
that deep
cleansing
breath

Will I?

WRITE

I'm a big believer in writing

Paint a picture with your words
Express your feelings as they come

See them and feel them

I do not desire to offend anyone
but
I will continue to write from my heart
as I generally do

I encourage you to do the same

I love the way Paul expresses his love for Christ Jesus
in his letters to the churches
I love how David gives voice to his anger
before God
without shame or fear
I love how Solomon describes his exquisite bride to be
the Shulamite

Write your thoughts

Write your feelings

Write your dreams, hopes, nightmares, and fears

Let your words flow through you
and onto the paper
pad
screen

Bottom line
write what you will

Don't be afraid

Picture

Sometimes it helps to look at the big picture
We see past ourselves
We see beyond what is lying before us
We may see the true nature of what is
We may even be able to see the beauty of what is to come
So much is blended and woven within
The eyes can no longer only focus on details
But gaze upon the myriad of picturesque colors before you

Sometimes it helps to look at the small picture
We see the finer points
We see the intricacy of what is
We see the smallest of a dot that
If left out
Would destroy the beauty
And change the meaning forever
We see the one color that stands out
Beyond all others
Signifying the strength and grace of solitude
We see the center
And all that encompasses and supports it
We see what must be
Because it is

FOR THE DREAMERS

Dream and never lose hope
DREAM
And dream some more

Follow
Chase
Capture your dream

Don't let your dream fade or dissipate

Find your dream
Live your dream

Let the passion of your dream carry you
Let your dream lead with passion

There is hope in our dreams
There are dreams in our hope

Dream my dreamers

Dream

Song of Falling Rain

The sky is dark and gray, and filled with falling rain
from the thick, heavy drops to a light drizzle
the rain comes to welcome the day

Like the keystrokes of a piano
or the plinking strings of the guitar
the rain falls in perfect cadence to form the song

Can you hear the rhythm
as the drops fall and collect into the melody
pooling together to pen the ballad

As the swaying chorus of the wind drifts
through the rain
the rain falls

And just as the sun begins to break through the clouds

It shines on the last note to end the song of falling rain

Inspiration to Write

Sometimes it's a feeling or a thought
sometimes it's that song that reaches deep inside
where the unseen can only be released
by piano key chords,
rhythms of guitars,
and the banging of drums.

It's the 4 minutes and 52 seconds of energy
beating through my heart
blood rushing through my head,
giving me tingles
through my arms and legs
sending them flailing through the air
like a wild man

Today is one of those days

THE ZAX

Not that either of them is in the right
But does it even matter
We, yes, we
We sit stuck
stuck in our ways
refusing to budge

A tiny sidestep here
or there

No way!

So, we
Yes, we
We sit
sit while the world moves
about and around us

How much pain do
We, yes, we
cause while sitting on our
self-righteous moral high ground
our principles

We

Yes, we

LOGICAL EMOTIONS

Not everything is black and white
But that also means
some things are

They just are

Why is it
that it was okay
to feel and express those deep emotions
in adolescence?

But now in adulthood

we're expected to be
so damn logical?

Crisis

Now is the time to be aware
Now is the time to open our eyes
see the pain that is around us

Now is the time to reach out
Now is the time to be supportive

Encourage, yes
but listen

Listen to their words
their heart

Listen to what is not spoken

Be that soft and safe place where someone can fall
empathize, rather than sympathize

Be what that person needs
and meet them where they are
not expecting them to change

Sit in their pain
their grief
and hurt with them

Don't fix

Listen

Pray

MUSIC

I think one of the greatest gifts God gave man
was music
It penetrates the heart
and moves the soul
It calms and comforts
Excites with tears of joy
Soothes the hurt and angered
Inspires the willing and unwilling
Praises its God and Maker

What a wonder gift

Thank you, God

Amen

Remembered

I listened
as the bow brushed across the strings

I remembered

I remembered the beauty of the song

so simple
so complex

peace
comfort
joy
contentment

Remembered

Certainty of Death

Death seems to be one of those things people
shrink away from and pretend it's not there

It is there and it cannot be ignored

There are times where every preparation can be made
but often it comes unexpectedly
even unwantedly

It can bring a family together with joyous
memories of love and fellowship
but death also breaks bonds
tears families apart with
unhealed wounds and regrets

Death often brings up long forgotten issues within us
issues that have not truly been dealt with
or perhaps healed superficially
only with a Band-Aid

And with each additional loss
hurt bubbles up to the surface of our hearts and minds

Rifts that were ignored and never mended
suddenly crack
open wide
with grief, hurt and anger

Regrets of missed opportunities
or of a lack of relationship
stare at the face of the distant one

Why do we allow this

How does the family dynamic
become so disdained that we push away

rather than embrace

What would it mean for each of us
to put aside our hurt
resentment
injustice
and give each other
and ourselves
grace

Would we be willing to forgive
even without an apology?

Will we choose to love
even if it is not reciprocated?

With the certainty of death
what will you choose?

THIS SONG

Music has often spoken the pain I cannot express
it goes to a depth that touches
beyond a place I am able to go

It's raw
authentic
a bit over the top at times
it feeds the feelings
that cannot seem to come out any other way

Right or wrong

In this moment
in this place
the song
speaks

Broken. Numb.
Antagonistic, angry silence
Unforgiven, unforgiving, indifference
Broken. Numb.

This moment

This place

This song

Spoke

For the Grief I Have Felt

There are so many things that could be said
about death, loss, and grief
Does anyone know just the right thing to say
Is there one phrase or statement
that encompasses all that needs to be said

As Christians can we simply say
death is not eternal and be done with it
What do we tell loved ones left behind
What do we say to the unbeliever
blinded from the Truth of God's Word

How do we relate or empathize

Can we
Will we

Death has a way of sharpening
edges of unresolved grief
Blades worn and dull
now cut the razor's edge
deep to the heart and soul
of our pain and loss

This ache knows no boundaries
it can capture us all

Death will come

and all,
in one way or another,
will come to this crossroad

Humbly search the depths of you
Examine grief

Your grief

THE MUSIC IN MY HEAD

Distracting sounds bounce across the wall
They float in and out of my view
Their high pitch laughter taunts me
Their squeals and crashes grate against my mind
Their tone, volume, and influx have me racing and chasing
The music of solitude in my head

The sweet solitude of silence
The calm contentment of nothing
Like notes dancing on a staff
They rest

Breathe deep
Deeper still
Feel the escaping air between my cold lips

Breathe deep
Deeper still
Hear the sweet sound of silence

Beating slowly
Slower still my heart

Shhh...

Quiet

---

[3] Fun fact about "The Music in My Head": I was feeling inspired to write and had my writing music on when all I could hear was Sponge Bob's annoying voice and laugh coming from the TV. I sat down to write about the music in my head, but when all I could hear was Sponge Bob, the poem took a different direction. The first stanza was me just free writing my frustrations of hearing his voice. At some point I realize the music in my head was actually silence. The silence was beautiful compared to Sponge Bob's laugh. From Breathe deep to the rest of the poem, I was trying to calm myself down. In the end I was telling myself (and Sponge Bob) to "Shhh," and "be quiet."

A Therapist's Heart

I choose joy
not for the pain I've been through,
but for the healing it will bring to others

With thankful heart
I walk the road no one wants to walk

Through eyes wide
I see the trauma behind closed souls
I hope for the hopeless
I hurt for the hurting

Joy, peace, and contentment
rage against the lies of
saddened depression
nervous anxiety
distressed suffering

Thankful truth twilights the path
that is beyond me
My path, for Your glory

I am a therapist

THE SPOKEN WORDS

I saw the impending swell
with its rolling approach

Inch by inch
it crept closer
moving
ever...
so...
slowly

The swell and tension building
like the final three ticks before a bomb

As if time stopped
the swell stood motionless
it towered over
as it waited to strike
taunting with fear

And then it happened

in the middle of a heartbeat
at the end of an exhale
time moved

Crashing down
came
lightning, thunder
the tsunami that hovered above

The spoken words,
"I want a divorce."

****

I don't know if it was a howl
or a scream
but it reverberated through the room

Like a six-inch needle
it stabbed

Like poison running through her blood
it penetrated every part
every bit of her body, mind, and soul

Simultaneously
I watched her knees buckle
and her face contort

She fell in slow motion
and yet,
at the speed of sound
anguish, pain, and suffering
wreaked havoc
as she wept and wailed
her hands balled into fists
pounded the floor
screams of terror fled her lungs

The spoken words,
"No! No! No! No!!!"

****

Stiff as a board
with Jell-O legs
he stood
shifting from one foot to the other
yet motionless

No words were spoken.
Well,
other than what was spoken

No tears
No angry outcry
No apparent emotion

A strange, awkward look on his face
maybe disbelief
maybe relief
perhaps both

His eyes shifted
from the floor beneath his feet
to the wailing, pounding, ball in front of him

To me

Flat affect

The spoken words,
"So, this is what it is like."

It's Just After Midnight: Christmas - 2018

The kids lay upstairs sleeping
all in one room, as tradition holds
all five of them
stretched out and squished
their steady breathing
in and out
dreams drift about

My wife finished the last-minute details
of the perfect setting
for our five

Exhausted and perhaps a bit overwhelmed
she is overcome with the abundant emotion
of awe

The day was long
but smiles were longer
The ever so sweet sound of her
not so silent breathing begins

It's peaceful downstairs
No sound can be heard
Well,
no sound but the rum pum-pum-pum
from the Little Drummer Boy

It fills the air and warms my heart
a steady beat, rhythm, and tempo sway
through and about me.

And as if in response
sudden drops of rain fall in perfect cadence

Minutes and seconds go by
maybe an hour

The music continues to play
The rain continues to fall
The inspiration continues to build
The peace continues to be

In a moment
it will all be over

The stairs will beckon me
and my not so silent breathing will begin
but in this one last moment
I will take solace

It is peaceful

It is hopeful

It is right

Acoustic

Like raindrops falling
through guitar strings strumming
softly
slowly
breathing in rhythm
gliding and sliding
floating and fluttering
dancing upon weightless time
endless
no beginning

That one sound
invigorates
inspires
intertwined with
hope and peace
present and future

The even flow
of the highs and lows
streams and dreams
like only I know

Peace and contentment
that joyous peace
everlasting

MY DAD'S GARAGE

Walking through my dad's garage you'll see all the tools I never learned to use. In his classic red rolling tool chest, there are the standard tools that tighten and loosen things, grip, grind, paint, pound, cut, smooth, and make holes. All the drawers are labeled. There is even a whole drawer dedicated to yellow number two pencils, freshly sharpened of course. With the top open, you'll see at least three levels and a couple tape measures. His metal work bench, which he got from his father-in-law's father, is stained with the memories of a billion projects.

Walking through my dad's garage, he is at home.

Walking through my dad's garage, I am lost.

I didn't learn how to use his tools in a proper manner. I didn't learn to build, fix, or create anything with his tools, other than a mess. My righty loosens and my lefty, left. My grip is weak, I grind nerves, my paint drips, I pound my fist, I cut corners. My talk is smooth, and I make holes in hearts. My pencils are black, dull, mechanical. My level is anything but, and my tape covers my eyes from truth. Stained is my body's workbench by the billions of projects I could not do. Like I said, walking through my dad's garage, I am lost.

For years I blamed my dad for not being an effective teacher.

For years I blamed myself for not being an attentive student.

The other day, I found myself walking through my dad's garage again. The feelings of shame and less-than crept up my spine and sank deep into my mind. Those all too familiar thoughts, beliefs, and lies stood before me: starring, taunting, accusing, blaming me.

That garage. That damn garage.

But then...

I thought about how easily a thin coat of paint can be chipped, like trust being chipped away. I remembered how my dad taught me to use a second coat of paint after letting the first coat dry. Like paint, we want to layer our trust over and over, so it thickens with strength and time.

I remember how my dad taught me to let wood soak up the stain before wiping it off or adding a second coat. This way the stain goes deeper, rather than simply staying at the surface. How many times in my life have I marinated in thought, feelings, or events in order to better understand? The richness of the stain is brought out with the varnish, but only after the deepening process. The richness of my life has only been after the stain, good and bad, has been processed through and accepted.

The polished finish beautifies my once stained heart.

How I enjoyed circling and squaring off the bushes outside the rose garden. Little by little a bush takes shape as the blade snips, clips, cuts, and chops. Leaves and branches pile higher and higher, making a terrible mess. That terrible mess, how I hated cleaning up that terrible mess. And yet, when I stood back and looked at the crisp corners and curves, the memory of what once was, faded. A smile stood where once the terrible chaos had just been. Twelve years of a terrible, chaotic mess. Twelve years of pruning. With tearful joy and grateful surprise, I stand outside the rose garden that is me. And I smile.

I never learned to weld, but iron sharpened iron and
welded the strength of my marriage.

I didn't know how to swing a hammer, but swaying to and fro,
my children slept in my arms.

I couldn't shape or mold wood, metal, or clay,
but the pressing of time shaped and molded my character
to the man standing before you.

Holes in the walls remained holes in my heart. Then one day, I saw you draw a line in the sand. With the flick of a Bic, you said no more. The roar of fire and flame set a new limit and boundary that would seal holes beyond my generation.

My dad's garage was unforgiving. The roots of stain deepen the pain of sorrow and resentment. Crushed was I by the sheer volume of anger, violence, and bitterness.

Yet, my dad became the living testament
of the very forgiveness I needed.
He showed me how to walk through his garage.

Forgiving the unforgivable

Even his garage.

---

[4] I started writing "My Dad's Garage" moments after my mom told me she had called 911 because he was unresponsive. I was at a beach birthday party for my in-laws. That was a hard day, but I LOVE what came out of it.

ORCHESTRA OF SILENCE

Silence is the code
Silence is the mode
Silent is the fight
The flight
And is the night

Racing, tracing, blistering pace
Strings and bows
Resound in place
Like rippling waves of grace
Silence falls upon my face

WHAT IF I'M NOT STRONG ENOUGH

Watching you fade away
slowing slipping
drifting
day after day

What if I'm not strong enough?

Holding you as you cry
holding my own river of tears at bay
as our kids hide from their own grief and fears

What if I'm not strong enough?

Answering questions I have no answers to
questioning answers I don't want
letting you go gentle into that good night
as I desperately cling to the hope of your day

What if I'm not strong enough?

Loving you enough to fight
loving you enough to rest
loving you more than me
loving you as God intended

What if I'm not strong enough?

Being present here and now
being present in the future
being present in your life
and when death does part us

What if I'm not strong enough?

Being a soft place for you to fall
being a rock for the kids to stand

Being the hope of testament for all to see

What if I'm not strong enough?

My heart pains and my mind spins
I don't want this

Please make it stop

I love you

What if I'm not strong enough?

TODAY WAS A BAD DAY

I woke to the harsh reality that is my future
Yes, it is future and has not happened yet
Ah, yet

Swimming through my mind
trying to control
Yet

That terrifying word yet

Yet has not come
Ah, but yet
yet will be

I laid there by your side and cried
not a sound, just
inverted screams echoing
in my silent tears

We cried
silently
no words

Dripping tears pooled
down our checks
soaked up by the pillow
beneath us

And then
whispers of forced air
release the relenting words,
"I am afraid."

I am so afraid
of losing you

I am so afraid
of what and how

Life will be after you are gone
So many fears
of what has not happened
yet

All the yets that are not yet

Yet
this was my day

It consumed me
my thoughts
my heart
my fear
my yet

Yet

EBB & FLOW OF LIFE

Breathe
Breathe deep
Breathe in the fresh flowers
The buzzing bees

Breathe
Breathe deep
Breathe in the rays of sun
The ocean waves

Breathe
Breathe deep
Breathe in the crunch of falling leaves
The crisp chill of cooling air

Breathe
Breathe deep
Breathe in the trickling rain
The flaking snow

Breathe
Breathe deep
Breathe in the beginning breath of life
The days, weeks, months, and years

Breathe
Breathe deep
Breathe in the here, the now, today
The later, the future, tomorrow

Breathe
Breathe deep
Breathe in the grief of passing
The dust to dust

Breathe
Breathe deep
Breathe in the ebb and flow
The what will always be

Today

I live and breathe my friend

Live...

and breathe

CHAPTER X

HOUSE OF MIRRORS

Often fascinated with the obscure, and certainly never wanting to be "normal", my mind takes me to some strange places. The rational and irrational swirl together to create illusions I question, yet revel in. In a maze of mirrors, the poet thinks, writes, and plays.

In Love with a Dream

A force beyond control
with false images
and false intentions

It takes you in
dominates your thoughts
comforts you
rationalizes your entire being

And at the precise moment
when you trust, care, and believe
everything you live for
is shot down and destroyed

Is it love or dream?

Love is without love
a satire
existing only in the poet's mind

Yes my lonely friend
the dreamer is here again.

Haunting in your sleep
he awaits you
his heart as ice
his mind as sword

And yes, his eyes
eyes of mirrors

The dreamer is here again

THE DREAMLESS SOUL

The enjoyment of a dream
can only be an illusion
a mirage of what we believe to be true
a dream
that is destined to die

Is it really necessary to dream?

I gaze into your eyes
and for the first time
I see me
as my eyes were once mirrors
so are the eyes of your soul
the soul that reflects only crystal
yet nothing is flawless

Could it be another fractured mirror?

I would then have to explain
and I know not how to
for the fracture is untouchable

All I Know...Lord

What's happening to me, Lord

Am I in another dream
living, breathing, seeing, and touching

Is it all just another dream

Perhaps a figment of my imagination
after all, isn't it all an illusion

I'm sorry Lord, I gave up dreaming

Remember?

It was too painful

It destroyed too much, including hope

All I know is
there is You

Me

And You

WRITER

In the past
I have prayed
That I might speak
As well as I write

But then

I would not be a writer

Hello – Goodbye

What's the difference
one's beginning and the other

Well, we all know the ending
to this story

Why hello when you have to say goodbye

Why say goodbye if you can't say hello

Tell me, do the two coincide

I'm a poet
which makes me a dreamer

So this concept of hello and goodbye
is a nightmare for me

Maybe it is the beginning to an end

I – WE

I wanted to write a poem
of love and dream
of evoking emotion

Instead
I wrote life

The heart, the soul, the mind
and the breath of our Lord
is the life we would share together

To have and to hold till death do us part

I
The lonely one
We
The only two

Was it all that complicated
or was it too simple to see

The heart filled with love
the soul with an eternity of peace
the mind captured with the memories
and future dreams

The breath from one
into another
giving a new life
for two to share
to become one
who writes a life of poems

A Breathing Satire

One in a thousand

Objective – to be that one
or to find the one

The poet creates in thought
transforms into words
as the mind races through empty voids

And then
the idea

The idea on paper

First one word, then two
a phrase here
a phrase there
page after page

A thousand to one
words, phrases, and pages
lead not to the idea

Soon the bleeding heart foreshadows
dreams in the mirror
only to not find
nor be
the one

Hiding Place

Well, Lord
it's back to my hiding place
sometimes
I wish I was not a poet

Then, Lord
maybe then, I could tell of my love

I could not only dream my love
But live my love

Rest

If only I could write

Then
and only then
would my mind
be at rest

LOST

I don't feel like writing
but I have to

I'm scared, confused, and frustrated
I don't know Lord

I feel I've failed already, again

There's a wall or block
I'm letting you down

My hope has lost faith
My trust, turned to fear
And insecurity

No resolve

No hope

Lost

The Unknown

Loving the known
Is the dream.
But I feel nothing near me.

Unknown are you,
To me.

You're but a drop of water
Among the sea,
Having you,
I would thirst no more.

To love you,
Is a dream.
To live without you,
Is a nightmare.

Reality is insanity,
And sanity is
My unknown.

SATIRE

And so
I dream on
and wake to death

What if I am already dead
and someone else is dreaming

No
I am alive

And dead
because I am
dreaming

Learn

Learn how to write

Love song
Poem
Thought
Story

Now that's a satire
Remember the breathing satire
Well, he's back

Deep in my head

Where to go

WRITER'S BLOCK

The start

Empty thoughts

Phrases and words racing

Through the mind

Nothing

TRAPPED

What am I to do, oh Lord?
I thought it was gone
But I guess I can't chase away love

She's everything I want
And yet, I am trapped
Trapped in this neverending friendship

Will my love shine through
Or will I hide
In the mask of friendship?

Will I ever truly know
Know her love?

Or will I suffer
In this dying mind of mine?

WHERE

Please tell me
someone
tell me
where did it go

The muse is gone
words are lost
the poet is sleeping

The bleeding hearts and artists

Where are they
amongst all
the lost dreams

Question

Is it possible to love too much
to dream too much
What if the love, the dream, and what appears to be
is bringing me closer to my own death

Could the very thing I desire most
lead to the death of me

Is the dream actually a nightmare

Illusion

Is the love truly love
or a distant mirage
tempting me
drawing me
luring me
to
my

Death

PHILOSOPHICALLY MISUNDERSTOOD

To be misunderstood
one needs
to understand himself
In some cases and situations
are we sure
we understand ourselves

I guess the real question is
How do we really know how we feel

Prime example
Love

How does one know
and explain
the feeling of being in love

Is it fair
to assume
you are in love

Is it fair to assume someone else is in love

This is where
one can be misunderstood

But only if he
himself
understands

EYES OF LOVE

My mind is racing
full of fury
My heart hurts
beckons for love

The games we are forced to play

Wow

I can't handle it anymore
I don't want to play

It is not worth it

The tears
pain
apathy

It is all worthless

The dream
mirror
poet

Her eyes

Eyes that burn
With love and fear

Foreshadowing future

Damn eyes

Colors of the Heart

The black
and the white
and yes
the gray.

The in-between
the unsure

The state of the unknown

Is the heart black and white
or is it too unknown by now

How can the heart be unknown

Does one not know

How they feel or think

Think?

Yes think
the mind has to

The heart feels
and the mind thinks

Is it possible for the two to conflict

Will they ever be black and white

Or will they remain endless and gray

The Poet's Mind

As the poet sits
in his abyss
mind racing with ideas

Thoughts. Dreams. Hopes.

A multitude of questions
followed by silent answers

His mind wanders off
to an old, familiar place
"Too many dreams"
whispers the air about him

Contentment with life
is what he needs
allusive dreams
is what he has
let the dreams fade away

His mind slips
into peaceful silence

CHAPTER XI

LOOKING GLASS

The other side.

Years of influence from family and friends has molded and shaped a side of me that is beyond me. A humble nod to them who loved, cared, and challenged me to be more than who I was in those moments. Their faces and mirrors will not be forgotten. They will live on in words and stories passed down through generations.

For My Children

My greatest desire
is to see
my children
come to the Lord

Dear God,
draw them to You
pursue them
bring them
to the foot of
the cross

Reveal Yourself to them
let them love You
and have a relationship
with You

Be their first love
their breath of life
their Abba Father
their Father God
their I AM!

AMEN!

I LOVE YOU

I once sang a song
A song of sorrow and loneliness
I knew something was missing in my life
I thought I knew what it was

I wanted to love and be loved
yet, this wasn't the link to happiness
I searched for what was missing
I did not know I was searching for you

Some may say it was fate
I know it was God's will

I found you on that glorious day
that missing link in my life
now found
now, I am complete

A new song is heard
a song of dreams and love
a song
simply entitled
I love you.

To Steve and Sandy
with love

I Can't Let Go

Crowded in a world of people
I was the lonely one
'til you came along

A friend was one thing
but you gave me a best friend
You were the one thing
the one feeling
I had never experienced before

I never thought I could love a friend
like I loved you

Our friendship was strong
but even stronger was time
and time, my friend, was the flaw in us

Changes in time
became me
you had no change
and soon, had no time

Words were said
words were ignored
and then one word,
"Bye."

To Pvt. David H. Cartwright
My heart is still with you

Looking in the Mirror

I once said
the eye is a mirror
a mirror is to look at
to wonder at
it is only a reflection
an imitation of an image

A mirror is only one way
but with two sides
an empty reflection
and the other
is pure darkness
together we see a reflection
empty darkness

Are these my eyes

A wise man once said,
"If his eyes are mirrors,
what is he looking at?"

The answer is obvious

His eyes are on the world
And he is blind

Dear God, please restoreth my sight

Thank you, Glenn "Allen" Christoph

MY FRIEND

Day by day I see you
Day by day we talk
We share, we listen,
We love

You are my day by day
And my night

You have enriched my life
With the joys you have given me
You have stood by my side
Through all the pain and sorrow

And when I needed you most
You knew what I needed
And simply smiled
And listened

You know my faults and downfalls
And yet you still love me

For all these things and more
I thank you and love you
For being my friend

THREE GENERATIONS

Lord, you have blessed me and saved me

You have given me this strange
powerful passion in life
You have broken down
the walls of my past
the walls of my heart
You have given me eyes to see over
and sometimes through
these walls in order to see You
Your light spills over the walls
caving them in
Thank You

Thank You for giving me my father back

Thank You for the timing
in which You spoke to him
and me

For years I wanted to know him
It was Your wisdom
and timing
that brought us together

Just as Your timing was so perfect
breaking that wall
I pray the wall
between my grandfather and I
may be taken down

I don't know how to love him
him, who hates me so much

I want to know and love him

I want him to know me
my wife
and his future great-grandchildren

Please dear Lord
Let this wall before me crumble down
Your light, grace, and love shining through

Thank You for wisdom, love, and timing
Amen

HAPPY 21ST B-DAY, STEVE

They say
now everything's legal
They say
"Now, you're a man."
If being a man
means doing everything
that is legal
I would rather be a child
and stay
in the tender arms of God

ODE TO MIKE STAND AND THE ALTAR BOYS

Time pressed my dance as
I went against the grain
I walked the wall

No doubt, I live in fallen world
My heart was lost in nowhere

I shouted louder, "I am a rebel!"
but I was broken
on the run

I needed mercy that lasted forever
and was more than words
I searched for the meaning of life
as I road that train

I am only human
and I stood alone
I cried, "Where's the new world?"

In the final hour I questioned it
but wanted more of You

Footsteps of love whispered in the morning
the gut level music
You are loved
Whether you stand or fall
I will melt into you

In the beginning and in the end
life begins at the Cross
and
I will follow You
Dear God!

Sibling Rivalry

At what point do our relationships
with our siblings
become so
disposable

As children we laugh and play
together

As adults
we ignore, shun,
chastise and belittle

How is it that our sibling relationships
can mean so little to us

Do you not miss your sister

Do you not long
to have your brother back

What will it take

New life
or perhaps

Death

When will your heart be opened
to the pain you're in

When will your eyes be opened
to the pain you've caused

Day after day
year after year
brick after brick

walls go up
higher and higher...

Justified in self-righteousness
your wall towers over you
blocking out your beloved sibling

Oh, to have peace in your heart
Oh, to have peace of mind
Oh, to have peace in the family

FRIENDS LONG AGO

I found an old U2 tape the other day

Listening to the music
my mind flooded
with memories of people and places
of long ago
A smile and a tear appeared before me
in my mirror

My heart pounded with exhilaration
as the kaleidoscope of pictures
raced by

Timeless faces
smiles
tears
they remain in my heart

For my friends long ago
will always be in my heart

SO NOT FADE, FADE, FADE AWAY...

Thank you for the memories

TIME

You've heard it said
there is a time for everything

Keep this truth to heart
in time
you will cherish
this time

For just as there is a time for everything

Everything takes time

The clock ticks
never stops
time goes on
and then this is done

Cherish your time
Live
in your time

Respect time

For in time
there is God

For Bryan Johnson

The Old Lamp

See the chips in the glass
and the rust in this old lamp

Our lives are like this lamp

Over the years we receive chips and nicks
At times we even rust or seem to fade
But in reality, this is when we shine the most
Our true selves are found in this light

May the light of this old lamp help you
to see things as they are
as they were
as they could be

May you see things at face value
but also as deep as the heart

May you see things from all sides
at every angle
and every curve

Let this lamp help you to see God

Let your eyes be open
And
See

For Debra Johnson – RIP

MOMMY, TELL ME A STORY

Son: Mommy, tell me a story.
Mom: Ok sweetie.
Love me tender, love me sweet...
Wait, did you brush your teeth?
Son: Oops, Ok...ready.
Mom: Love me tender, love me sweet,
I'm going to tickle your feet!
Son: No mommy, no. Tell me a real story.
Mom: Okay. I know just the one.

Once upon a time...

Vinyl after vinyl dropped
Music echoed through the house
As the music played
The walls shook with anticipation and joy
They danced and swayed
To the resounding rhythm and rhyme
Their outstretched mouths sang along
"I Love It Loud," the walls shouted
With pounding and ringing ears

This is what they heard...

My teddy bear was all shook up
when she couldn't help falling in love
with a hound dog

They wrote love letters
from viva Las Vegas to Blue Hawaii
but from its blue moon
it rained in Kentucky
They were paralyzed with big love
big heartache

Teddy Bear had a suspicious mind
about a brown eyed girl
yet still stuck on you

Love me tender in the garden led to
Teddy Bear's heartbreak hotel
Lonesome tonight
the Hound Dog sat in jailhouse rock
and there was no more peace in the valley
All my letters were returned to sender

Who am I without you
they both wondered

Hound Dog was way down
his blue eyes crying in the night
he howled,
"Don't be cruel and don't leave me now.
Please don't run away. You don't have to say you love me
but what do you want me to do?
You're the devil in disguise,
but you're young and beautiful and my good luck charm.
If tomorrow never comes for such a fool as I,
I'll remember you...my wooden heart... moody blue."

In the early morning rain
Teddy Bear whimpered,
"Why me Lord?
I hurt without my boy, my tiger man.
I'm so lonesome I could cry.
I am indescribably blue.
Hound Dog, I'm trying to get to you and it's now or never.
I just can't help believing in the wonder of you.
There's a honky-tonk with G.I. blues
so, kiss me quick and let's rock a hula baby."

"All I wanted was a little more conversation
from my big hunk o' love," Teddy Bear cried.

"The wonder of you became my way
and my burning love," sang Hound Dog.

Thinking about you
because you are always on my mind
Teddy Bear sang
the love song of the year

I can dream of you forever my darling
When my blue moon turns gold
there will be no more blue Christmas
Welcome to my world CC rider
let's run on to the promise land
to the white Christmas

You help me
You love me
You gave me a mountain

What now my love
It's only you, my angel

So, crying in the chapel
wearing blue suede shoes
they committed to stand by each other
in their Father's House
through the by and by

Son: Thank you mommy. That's my favorite story.
And mommy, I just can't help falling in love with you.

Mom: Thank you sweetie.
I love you to the blue moon and back.

Happy Mother's Day, Mom!

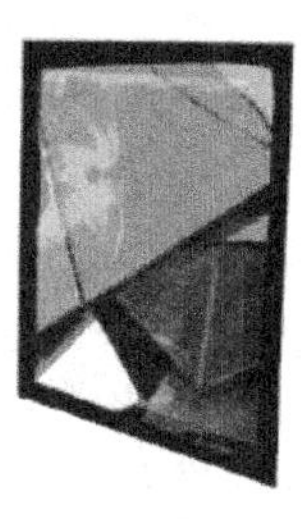

CHAPTER XII

IMAGE OF GOD

I love giving praise to my Lord, God, and Savior Christ Jesus. I will forever be thankful for God's sacrifice in giving His Son to die for the penalty of sin. I will forever be thankful for Christ Jesus's birth, death, and resurrection so that we may live with Him and our Father God for all eternity.

I believe He is the One True God and I want all to know Him.

I love giving praise to my Lord, God, and Savior Christ Jesus!

Christmas 2009

In one
magnificent
Holy
humble moment

Jesus was born

In that moment
the world changed

In that moment
all eyes would forever turn to Him

IN THAT MOMENT...

BIRTH TO ETERNAL

The Lord your God
created you in His image and likeness
He looked upon you
and proclaimed
every man, woman, and child as
very good

The Lord your God
commands you to be
righteous, holy, and virtuous

Children of God
hear these words
hold them to your heart

The Lord your God loves you
He sent His Son
to die for you
so you may live
in Him
forever

May the Lord
your God
bless you
and keep you

Saved

My God,
my Savior,
my Abba-Father
thank you for Your image

Thank you
for sending Your Son
and sacrificing Him
for us...for me

My dear sweet Jesus,
thank You
for Your obedience
Your love
Your perfect image

All my sins
past
present
future
are forgiven

At the Foot

Can you see the star
Is there someone or something that brings you
To the tiny feet of the baby Jesus

Are you searching

Is your heart longing
Pounding

Is your knee bowed
Humbled

Is your tongue confessing
Praising

Merry Christmas

Yes,
Christmas!

Palm Sunday

Torn between the anger
grief and sadness
of The Fall

And of my sins

And
the peaceful joy
of the everlasting life
I have received
through the
life
death
resurrection
of my Savior

Christ Jesus

For His glory
Christ gave His life
that we may be saved

Do you believe?

FRIDAY

It's Friday
But Sunday's comin'
Do I dare let myself dwell upon Friday

Can I accept the pain that He endured for me
The sacrifice

It's Friday
I am so sorry
I hate that it was my sin
Our sin
That put Him on the cross

Dear God
Please forgive me
It's Friday
And my God freely gave Himself for me

For us

It's Friday
But Sunday's comin'!!!

Tomorrow is Easter

Tomorrow is
what sets our lives
and our world
apart

Tomorrow the stone was rolled away

Tomorrow my Savior rose

Yesterday, today, tomorrow
and forever
Christ Jesus lives

This is my Savior
All are welcome

Every knee shall bow
and tongue confess
Jesus Christ is Lord

All are welcome

Come
Believe
Praise Him

This is my Jesus

EASTER

I know not everyone believes as I do
I also know that I walk a fine line
between sharing my faith
and offending

My desire and intention
is not to offend anyone
but this is my faith

I am not ashamed
I truly believe
Christ Jesus is the only way to God
And my heart aches
for those who don't believe

It is not about intolerance
It is about the love
Jesus willingly gave
and gives us

It is about the Savior who
gave His life
so that we may live

Please, do you believe?

Johnny Cash

Think about this for a second
If the man in black believed in Jesus
Can you

Cash was a drunk
an adulterer
and, at times, a violent man

AND YET

In the end
he died
knowing that he would spend
eternity with his Lord Christ Jesus

Imagine that
The man in black
in heaven

The blood of Christ knows
no boundaries
has no limits
and will make the vilest heart clean
pure

The man in black believed

Will you?

THANKSGIVING 2009

I am thankful for my God, my Savior, my Abba Father
who sent His Son to live, to die and be risen from the dead
so we may have eternal life with Him

I am thankful for the humble obedience of Jesus Christ
in following His Father's will

I am thankful for His sacrifice

I am thankful that Christ Jesus
lived
died
and rose
on the third day

I am thankful for the shed blood of my Savior, Christ Jesus
which covers my sins
from before I was

All my sins were forgiven
(past, present, and future)

I am thankful there is nothing
that can separate me from the love of God
which is in Christ Jesus

I am thankful that
on the third day
Christ Jesus rose from the dead
and ascended into heaven
to be with His Father

I am thankful for the Holy Spirit

Who was sent by Christ Jesus to live within me

I am thankful
for on that day
when I die
I will spend eternity
with my God
My Savior
My Abba Father!

One Day, Week, Month, Year

How many lives could be saved
How many hearts could be broken
How many hearts could be mended

How many babies will be born
How many lives will be lost

How many minds will be inspired
How many miles will be traveled
How many flowers will bloom

How many days, minutes, seconds will be wasted

How many will kneel before the King
How many will proclaim the name of Christ Jesus

How many will reject Him

How many will cry out in
Praise, prayer
Desperation, tears, anger, loneliness
Obedience, faithfulness, humility
Honor, respect, and awe

How many...

CHRIST JESUS

What is in a name
Why is His name so special
Why is His name so loved
Why is His name so hated, despised, and rejected
Why is His name *Emmanuel* (God with us)

Could it be that Christ Jesus is everything
He claimed to be
He is the great I Am
The Son of God
The Savior of all mankind
The Creator of everything that has been and will be created

The Savior

He is God
He and the Father are one
He is the Alpha and Omega
He is I Am
Emmanuel
God with us

I will celebrate my God, my Savior, my Christ Jesus
He is God with us
There is nowhere we can go where He is not
God with us

He is
Always has been
Always is
Always will be

God with us

BREATH OF HEAVEN

God breathed
And gave Adam the breath of life
God breathed again
Doing the same for Eve

The Spirit of God fell upon Mary
God breathed
And His Son was born

The Creator
Of all that was, is, and is to come
Breathed life
Life of the Living God
Into Mary
So that His Son
Christ Jesus may live among us

What other wonders can His breath do
Breath of heaven
Fall on me
Let me know
Your will

Thank you, my dear God and Savior

HANDEL'S MESSIAH

It speaks to the mystery of Christ
His love
His glory
His Kingship
His Kingdom
His power
His worthiness

His identity as the Savior
of all that would receive Him
Since by man came death
should it not then be
by Man (Christ Jesus)
that all be made alive

Not out of fear
but out of love
Christ Jesus came

Not out of fear
but of love
I accepted Him

Not of fear
but out of love
will I follow
my Savior Christ Jesus

For Unto Us

For unto us a Child was born
For unto us this Child lived
preaching Truth
in love
For unto us
this Child
pointed the way to God

For unto us
this Child
paid the penalty for our sin

For unto us
this Child
became the living sacrifice
for all that would come to Him

For unto us
this Child
is the new covenant

For unto us
this Child
is the Way, the Truth, and the Life

For unto us
this Child
is the Great I Am

For unto us
Christ Jesus

Christmas Eve 2013

Glory in the highest belongs to
The One and Only Son of God
Christ Jesus

I'll admit
It's hard to grasp
All glory belonging to Him

He is the Creator of all
That is
That was
That will be created

His glory knows no bounds

Even the nature of Himself
Pours out glory to Him

All glory
All worship
All praise
Be to our King
Our Lord
God
Savior

Christ Jesus
He is glory
He is I Am

Christmas 2013

Worthy is the Lamb!

Today we celebrate His birth

Never was there
a more defining change in man's life
than the birth of Christ Jesus,
until His death and resurrection

May we never forget
without the death and resurrection of Christ Jesus
His birth would be just as any other

It is through His death and resurrection
we may live eternally

Thank you
Abba Father
for sacrificing Your Son
for our sake

Hope For Everyone

There is hope in many things
but our truest hope comes from Christ Jesus
He is the hope for anyone, everyone, all
It's not foolish or weak to hope in Him

There's hope for everyone

Bring your brokenness
hurt and pain
Bring your depression
anxiety and trauma
Bring your anger
frustration and rage

There's hope for everyone

Bring your joy, peace
your contentment
Bring your happy
sad, mad
Bring your tears
fears and jeers

There's hope for everyone

On your knees
On your feet
Head raised
Head bowed

There's hope for everyone

Shout or whisper
through clenched teeth
or jaws wide
desperate, hopeless, and helpless

humble

with all respect and reverence

There's hope for everyone

Dear Little One

Your heart will be broken by man, woman, and child
Your sight will be blinded with greed, lust, and self
Your mind will split by evil and detestable thoughts
Your ears will resound with the world
Your mouth will speak the foulest of words of disdain and Hate
Your body will be beaten and defiled
Your actions will be horrific and shameful

All the while, I will be with you
I will walk with you shoulder to shoulder
I will lead you where I need you to go
I will lift you up and carry you when you are too weak
I will even sit with you, beside you
In whatever and every moment you need Me

My Spirit will dwell in you
My Spirit will never depart from you
My Spirit will be with you everywhere, always

You cannot run from Me
You cannot hide from Me
You cannot lose Me
I will always be with you

Yell, scream, cry...
I Am with you.
Cheer, squeal, laugh...
I Am with you.
Even in your silence...
I Am with you.

I Am your Lord, God, and Savior
I Am the Creator
Of all that is, was, or will be
I Am Light and Truth
I Am God, The Father
I Am Christ Jesus, The Son
I Am Counselor
I Am your Abba Father
I Am

Your heart will be mended, healed, and made anew
Your heart will rejoice with such love
You cannot fathom
Your sight will be on Me and My glory and honor
You will see My love for you, firsthand
Your mind will be filled with Truth
Your mind will be captivated with what is lovely and pure
Your ears will hear My still small voice AND My lion's ROAR
Your ears will hear the music of My heart
Your mouth will sing My praises
Your mouth will confess, I Am Lord
Your body will be healed and righteous
Your body, once sacrificed, will now be holy and clean
Your actions will be true, and right
Your actions will be on bended knee, for Me

Yell, scream, cry...
I Am with you.
Cheer, squeal, laugh...
I Am with you.
Even in your silence...
I Am with you.

Dear little one
I chose you before you were born
I chose you before the dawn of man
I chose you before there were stars in the sky
Before the earth had form
Even before there was light
I chose you before time was
Before there was

I wrote your name in My Book of Life
I engraved My name in your heart
I engraved your name in My hand
I put My seal upon your forehead
Never broken, damaged, or removed

Yell, scream, cry...
I Am with you.
Cheer, squeal, laugh...
I Am with you.
Even in your silence...
I Am with you.

My dear little one
I love you

Acknowledgments

Laurie: My shining light, my true north, my beautifully imperfect! For thirty years now, I've had the joy and honor of knowing and loving you. I've never loved anyone as deeply or passionately as I love you. You are my True Love Ways.

Thank you for loving me, laughing with me, crying with me, and yes, even fighting with me.

For years you told me, "I can't wait for you to see what I see in you." Thank you for seeing more in me than just a fractured mirror. Thank you for seeing the beautifully imperfect man God created me to be. Patiently you waited as the dim light grew to the brilliant light of the Son. With a multitude of "Aha!" moments (and many more to come), I see. Thank you! As we walk this unknown road of cancer, I will be with you every step of the way. I will never want to let you go, but I know the Lord is calling you home. When that day comes, I will be there with you, holding your hand and humbly giving it to our Father God in heaven.

I promise to continue to honor you by doing what is right by our children.

Emma, Zachary, Michael, Matthew, and Aubrey: My five little monkeys. Thank you for loving me, as fractured as I still am. Thank you for being authentic, sharing your heart and laughter in your poems. I am beyond proud of you!

Mom and Dad: Your love, encouragement, and support through the years influenced both the dark and light within me. Above all, you exhibited true change and brought me hope.

Rikah: Thank you for your guidance and belief in me. Thank you for your never-ending encouragement while walking me through the process. You proved my dream was more than just a dream, but real, tangible, and flesh & blood. You showed me it can be done and done well. Thank you for hearing my pain, allowing me to live in it and write in it, but not dwell in it. From authentically me to authentically you, here's to the "one-minute clinics." Thank you, Rikah!

Tiffany: I wanted an editor who was willing to be direct, critically honest, tell me, "No" and also be willing to listen, knowing this is my dream. You surpassed each of these expectatons, amplifying my voice to what it is today. Thank you for encouraging me to stretch further, not constraining my poetry, but truly opening up to the imagery it was naturally producing.

Sharon: Thank you for taking the time to hear my vision, story, and purpose. Thank you for seeing what I could not see and making it better than what was already in my head. For years I dreamt of this cover, but it was only fuzzy until you made it crystal clear.

Rikah, Kolleen, Heather, Jennifer, and Kamiah: Thank you for the time you spent beta reading and proofreading *Fractured Mirror: Beautifully Imperfect.* Your comments, critiques, corrections, and questions were instrumental.

Thank you for your honest opinions. I value how you continued challenging me where I need to be challenged. You each brought a different strength and view and I will forever appreciate your hard work. Thank you.

God: Father God, thank You for creating me to be me and loving what You created.

SPECIAL THANKS

J.B., Tenacity, faith, and humility brought your work to life. Behind the scene and unknown to you, you were and are an inspiration to me.

J.C., Your stories and desire to entertain your readers inspired me to remember the reader and how important they are, and yet, still allow myself to write for myself.

J.A., Your characters are written into life through the flesh and blood you give them with your words. Your care for them as if they were real. Your talent inspired me to reach deeper in order to add flesh and bone to my work.

H.J., You are a metaphor genius! Your angst, passion, and boldness inspired new voice and life in me. Invaluable!

Thank you to you four. Your words influenced me, but it was your passion that truly inspired me. I will forever think of you and be inspired by you!

FROM THE AUTHOR

Thank you for reading my book, *Fractured Mirror: Beautifully Imperfect*, and helping my dream to come true. I am honored and humbled.

God designed each of us with a multitude of emotions. I felt an abundance of them over the last two years of putting this book together. It seemed like a billion "what if" questions plagued me through each step, but no more.

I hope you were moved and touched by these poems and prose. From the dreamy to the darkness and grief, to the hope and love, I pray you allowed yourself to experience the fullness of life as you read.

At the same time, I pray your rationale was challenged or perhaps reinforced. I believe the logical thought process we each go through needs to be challenged, reevaluated, and reinforced regularly. Our thoughts need to go deeper than the mundane of our daily routine or the surface level of our existence.

Life is full of emotions, and often they are irrational. Often, they carry us to the outer realm of our own existence and just do not make any sense. I've learned to be okay with that and even embrace it at times. Your journey is your journey. Let it take you where you need to go.

Let us question what we've known or what we don't understand,

and, through that questioning, gain a more profound relationship with those around us and ourselves.

Learn to appreciate your life, loved ones, and those around you in the joyous times and in the dark trials. Live your life in the Truth. The glass IS half full AND half empty.

Final thoughts and prayers for you:

Numbers 6:24-26 New American Standard Bible (NASB)
May the LORD bless you, and keep you;
The LORD make His face shine on you,
And be gracious to you;
The LORD lift up His countenance on you,
And give you peace.'

Psalm 139:7-12 New International Version (NIV)
Where can I go from your Spirit?
Where can I flee from your presence?
If I go up to the heavens, you are there;
if I make my bed in the depths, you are there.
If I rise on the wings of the dawn,
if I settle on the far side of the sea,
even there your hand will guide me,
your right hand will hold me fast.
If I say, "Surely the darkness will hide me
and the light become night around me,"
even the darkness will not be dark to you;
the night will shine like the day,
for darkness is as light to you.

Philippians 4:8-9 New International Version (NIV)
Finally, brothers, whatever is true, whatever is noble, whatever is right, whatever is pure, whatever is lovely, whatever is admirable—if anything is excellent or praiseworthy—think about such things. Whatever you have learned or received or heard from me, or seen in me—put it into practice. And the God of peace will be with you.

Made in the USA
Coppell, TX
01 September 2020